Mind Morphing
- Decision Making using Logic and Magic

by John Rayment

PUBLICATIONS LIMITED

© Copyright remains the property of the named authors.
© Copyright of the animation remains the property of B. Pierce. All rights reserved. No reproduction, copy or transmission of this publication may be made without written permission.

Any person who carries out any unauthorised act in relation to this publication may be liable to criminal prosecution and civil claims for damages.

While the publisher and editors have made every effort to ensure that the contents of this publication are accurate, responsibility can not be accepted for any errors.

First published in September 2001

ISBN 1-900-432-30-7

Published by

Earlybrave
PUBLICATIONS LIMITED

Printed in the United Kingdom by
**The
PRINTING
PLACE ltd...**

Authors:
John Rayment

John Rayment spent the first eight years of his working life as a management accountant in a variety of public sector organisations. For the last twenty years, he has been in business education, management and consultancy:

- Financial Management and Human Resource Consultant to small and large businesses.
- Lecturer at Monash University, New Victoria, Australia.
- Managing Director of a successful training company.
- Business Development Manager at the Ashcroft International Business School in the UK.

John has written books on business financial management, decision making, human resource management and management accounting, and presented papers at several international conferences.

Dedication

Silently fighting
Day after day
Trapped inside watching
Your building decay
Forced to a mumble
Defiant you say:
"If there is a God...
There must be a way"

Silently helping
Day after day
Trapped beside watching
Your lover decay
True dedication
Cheerful you stay
Screaming inside: "God,
There must be a way"

Silently sharing
Day after day
Trapped outside watching
Your lives ebb away
How can we help you?
Frustrated we pray:
"Logic or Magic, God
Show us the way"

Content
Chapters

	Page
1. Introduction	1
2. Problem Solving	17
3. Decision Making	75
4. Risk Management	115
5. Mind Games	139
6. Groups	219
7. A Combined Approach	253

Chapter 1
Introduction

You have 2 things to worry about:

Are you rich?
Or are you poor?

If you are rich, you have nothing to worry about
If you are poor, you have 2 things to worry about

Are you healthy?
Or are you ill?

If you are healthy, you have nothing to worry about
If you are ill, you have 2 things to worry about

Will you get better?
Or will you get worse?

If you will get better, you have nothing to worry about
If you will get worse, you have 2 things to worry about

Will you live?
Or will you die?

If you will live, you have nothing to worry about
If you will die, you have 2 things to worry about

Will you go to heaven?
Or will you go to hell?

If you will go to heaven, you have nothing to worry about
If you will go to hell..
you will be so busy shaking hands with all your friends...
you won't have time to worry!

"Don't worry, be happy!"

While this saying is comforting, as indicated in the dedication, it should not be taken too seriously. In both our business and private lives we are constantly faced with decision making and problem solving, from the crucial to the trivial.

Crucial business decisions may include product selection, development and pricing; resource allocation; staff selection, training and retention; and design of a new building. A trivial one could be the colour of the curtains in that new building.

Note that a decision that may at first sight appear to be unimportant can in fact be vital, particularly if made badly. Who makes the tea, and what time is the lunch break, are two possible examples. If the same person is always 'nominated' as tea maker, or forced to take their break at an unpopular time, they may feel undervalued, or even insulted. A possible claim of discrimination could result. Even the curtain colour may be crucial to those who believe in Feng Shui, or in the Board Room at a football team's ground!

Our private lives are full of such issues as where to live, how to stay healthy and generate 'loads'a money', and which video to watch whilst eating what for dinner? You can hopefully see that some of them will be more important than others, but that will depend on the potential consequences — what is eaten could be life threatening to someone with a nut allergy.

This book outlines the decision making process in general and its application in our business and private affairs. A companion book, Mind Management, looks at ways in which we can develop our minds, partly to improve our decision making / problem solving, but also because a top quality brain is a nice thing to have!

Physical fitness is often measured in 3 ways, strength, stamina and suppleness, and it is generally accepted that regular exercise can help improve and maintain such fitness. I believe the same applies to the mind, and the companion book attempts to show ways you can improve your mental strength, stamina and suppleness. I know you probably want to rush straight out to buy the other book and start getting mentally fit, but an important part of decision making is to not allow yourself to be easily side-tracked, so stick with this one for now.

Logic and Magic

The two basic styles of decision making covered herein are Logical and Magical, and I will demonstrate them by considering the following problem:

> *119 players enter a knock out singles tennis tournament. How many matches will be required?*

If you are to benefit fully from this book, it is vital that you attempt the problems before seeing the answers, otherwise you will find yourself reading the answers and thinking 'that's obvious' when in fact you might not have adopted the same approach at all. Hopefully, you will occasionally (but not too often!) find a better 'solution' than the one provided: I make no claim that my approach is always best, and very often there will be several ways to tackle the same problem, each of which may have its own merits.

Your own thoughts, ideas and attempted solutions to the problems discussed will be valuable when you come to review particular points or apply them to real problems of your own. If you do find any clearly superior approaches, better / alternative illustrations or examples, can't understand part of the book, or would just like to express an opinion, I would be very pleased to hear from you, my e-mail address being j.j.rayment@apu.ac.uk.

So do not turn the page until you have worked out, or at least spent some time thinking about, the answer to the above problem. Either use the space provided below or an exercise pad of your choice. Don't worry about writing in the book — it is not a limited edition work of art, and you can always buy a second copy. If you have nothing handy to write with do ten knuckle press-ups for not being prepared, and try to work it out in your head, which will be very useful practice and a good start to your mental fitness programme.

Logical

A person adopting a logical approach tends to:

- use a system or model for problem solving
- consider each step of the problem in turn
- justify solutions by the approach used
- define constraints as early as possible
- discard alternatives as early as possible
- constantly review the situation until a solution "appears"
- – or the problem changes to fit the solution!

An extreme variation of this approach is scientific / mathematical theory, in which each step of a solution must be solved before the next step is taken.

Scientific/Mathematical Approach

One logical approach to the tennis tournament problem would be as follows:

Round	Number of Players	Number of Matches	Players Still In After This Round
First	118 (1 player has a bye)	59	59 + 1 = 60
Second	60	30	30
Third	30	15	15
Fourth	14 (1 bye)	7	7 + 1 = 8
Fifth	8	4	4
Sixth	4	2	2
Seventh	2	1	1 (the winner!)
Add the matches		**118**	

Many variations exist, each of which should give the correct answer. In practice, the first round would usually be used to reduce the number of players to a power of 2 i.e. 2, 4, 8, 16, 32, 64, 128 etc., so that no byes would be necessary in subsequent rounds. In this case, 55 matches would be required in the first round to reduce the players still in the tournament to 64. The full analysis would then be:

Round	Number of Players	Number of Matches	Players Still In After This Round
First	110 (9 byes)	55	55 + 9 = 64
Second	64	32	32
Third	32	16	16
Fourth	16	8	8
Fifth	8	4	4
Sixth	4	2	2
Seventh	2	1	1 (the winner!)
Add the matches		**118**	

Magical

A person who uses (or appears to use) magic in problem solving tends to:

- keep the total problem in mind
- continually redefine the problem as they learn about it
- look at the problem from a number of different viewpoints
- consider alternatives / options simultaneously, often as packages
- "feel" whether an approach is correct
- be keen to experiment with solutions
- hop about between ideas and parts of the problem
- make very fast evaluation of alternatives

A term I use for this approach is **MAGICAL MIND GAMES (MMG)** or often just mind games. It is more akin to playing with a problem than tackling it in a logical progression of steps, extreme variations being trial and error or guesswork. The magical side comes from the fact that, as with more traditional forms of magic, to the observer, the solution often seems to just appear, or be some kind of a trick, while to the magician there is a logical explanation. With Magical Mind Games, the magic is often even stronger, with the magician being as surprised as anyone when the solution appears, often from the least expected places.

Most of the time once the solution is found, its validity and logic are obvious and people are amazed that they did not see it before. It is interesting to note that many major scientific breakthroughs have first come to a person either by luck / fluke, in a dream, or by a sudden flash of inspiration as if by magic. Validity of the solution often has to be confirmed or proved by logical, systematic analysis, but the inventor / discoverer often "knows" instinctively that they have found the right answer. Examples of this kind of success are discovery of the Periodic Table in chemistry, penicillin, smallpox vaccine and the wheel. Do you know of any others?

If you didn't realise I just 'invented' the wheel example, you should be more thoughtful about what you read! How could I possibly know? It may have been discovered by logical thought about physics and applied mathematics, but my guess is it was more by thoughtful application and experimentation following a lucky observation. This may have been made by someone who accidentally trod on a pebble or other spherical object and had their feet rolled away from under them.

An MMG approach to the tennis problem would be to look at it from another angle i.e. to realise that each player will lose once (and only once) except for the winner. Thus, we need one match less than the number of players i.e. 119 - 1 =118.

This is typical of a mind games solution - as stated above, they are often obvious, logical and simple once you see them, and can make you feel very stupid and frustrated if you have just spent ages working out the answer using a more complicated approach. The problem was deliberately selected to illustrate the point that we can easily become hooked into using certain approaches when other much simpler ones may exist. Mind games is really all about finding the best approach to a solution, be it logical or other. If the question had been "How many rounds will be required?" it is hard to see how MMG could improve on the following standard logical analysis. (What I should have said is "it is hard for me to see...". You may be able to see an alternative approach which is a great improvement - don't allow my failure to put you off).

The table prepared for the logical approach showed a requirement for 7 rounds. Working back from the final it can be seen that one round copes with two players, two rounds up to four, and each extra round doubles the number of potential players. So to find how many rounds are required, we just start at one and see how many times we have to keep doubling until we include the target number of players.

Maths!

This can be verified mathematically using powers. If you are an "I don't do maths" person, and immediately recoiled in horror on reading that sentence, at least see if you can follow the basic ideas being expressed. Attempting things you are not particularly good at helps keep the mind flexible, very important when using MMG, and you might surprise yourself by discovering that you do do maths after all! (I can dream). If you try but still fail, 'don't worry, be happy': there are mathematical parts in the book, but don't let them put you off. They are not vital and I have written the book with the intention that it can be understood with or without the maths. Give the maths a try, but if it leaves you cold - possibly with the hair on your neck standing up, clammy hands, and sweat running down your back - just go back to the original, non-mathematical explanations and thank God for computers.

Each time we double, we are multiplying by 2, so we are looking at powers of 2. If we double up three times, we will have multiplied our original number of players (i.e. 1) by 2x2x2 = 8. Expressing 2x2x2 as a power, we say 2^3, and up to 8 (but above 4 which would only take 2 rounds) players requires 3 rounds. 32 is 2x2x2x2x2 = 2^5, and up to 32 (but above 16 which would only take 4 rounds) players requires 5 rounds. In general, n rounds would be required for any number of players up to and including 2^n, but above 2^{n-1}. 119 lies between 64 and 128 i.e. between 2^6 and 2^7, so 7 rounds are needed.

Structure

This chapter was intended to give you an idea as to the content and style of the book, and whet your appetite for more. I hope it has done so.

Introduction

Chapters 2 to 4 look in more detail at using a logical approach to problem solving, decision making and risk management respectively. Chapter 5 identifies potential weaknesses in that approach, and ways of tackling them, before going on to look in detail at the use of Magical Mind Games. Chapter 6 looks at the desirability of involving other people in our problem solving, and ways of ensuring this is done effectively, while chapter 7 concludes the book by detailing and illustrating an approach to decision making / problem solving which draws on all the knowledge and techniques used throughout.

Little Ms Majik thinks this is all wrong, with far too much emphasis being placed on the old fashioned logical approach. She thinks most people will be bored stiff with that and never get to the interesting Magical Mind Games part. I tried to tell her that is not fair on Sir Lancelot, the logical approach has much in its favour, and in any case people need to understand the logical approach and its weaknesses if they are to fully appreciate MMG, but she wasn't impressed or amused.

Then I hit on an MMG solution: challenge the assumption that a book should be read from front to back, and let the readers decide for themselves! So, over to you: if you feel Little Ms Majik is right (her name should tell you that she is biased) why not start with chapter 5? Or, if you would rather, start with Sir Lancelot and his approach in chapter 2. Whichever you decide, I hope you enjoy the book and find it useful and thought-provoking.

At the end of each chapter you will find self-test questions to use to confirm your basic understanding of points made in the text, and encourage you to think about them, and exercises to use to practice the techniques covered in the chapter. These are followed by guideline answers to the exercises.

The final question challenges you to use your newfound skills to solve the biggest problem facing mankind . . .

Self-Test Questions

1.1 Differentiate between logical and magical approaches to decision making. Are the two approaches completely different, or do they overlap?

1.2 Think about some decisions you have made recently. Was your approach basically logical, magical, a combination of the two, or something completely different? Did your approach work well? Can you see how a different approach might have worked better?

Exercises

1.1 MARBLES
How many matches are required if 47 players enter a knock-out marbles competition?
How many rounds?

1.2 ANAGRAMS
Unscramble the following SPORTS / PASSTIMES:-

i. E S T L B A E T N I N
ii. L W O R E P A O T
iii. R L I S D B L I A
iv. N T O B M A I D N
v. K E O H Y C
vi. T G I S R W E L N
vii. E C Q T O U R
viii. R Y H A E C R
ix. E K C T I R C
x. C A H E T I L T S
xi. A D Y S E W P E
xii. N O H I S T O G
xiii. K B L A T L B E S
xiv. I L U N C G R
xv. K I Y D L D T S W N I
xvi. R C O S L S E A
xvii. E D I S O M N O
xviii. M G S I W N I M
xix. G A R H D U S T
xx. G N Y C I L C

1.3 GETTING RESULTS

Background
You are the course leader for some courses run at Angle Iron University. It is Tuesday 6.00pm and the Examinations Board has just finished approving the results.

The Head of School, located at another campus some 50 miles away, has requested that you provide her with a set of the results by 8.00am the next morning, in time for an important meeting.

Required
You are required to select the most appropriate method of getting the results to the Head of School.

Other information
Train
? via London ;
? your campus is very close to the local station, but the other is some 4 miles from its nearest one, although between 6.00a.m. and 10.00p.m., buses run hourly between that station and the campus;
? cost - train (return) £15.40
   - bus: station to campus (single) £1
?   journey time (each way) - train 90 minutes
                              - bus   10 minutes

Coach
? every 3 hours, from 5.30a.m. to 8.30p.m.
? the coach drop off is half a mile from the annexe
? cost would be £3.30 (return) and journey time 110 minutes

Car
? you can drive but following a recent accident your car is not available
? a pool car is free for use on Wednesday at a charge to the School of 60p per mile
? journey time would be 70 minutes

The university's last post collection is 5.30pm.

Answers to Exercises

1.1 MARBLES

Using Magical Mind Games
47 competitors, 1 winner, so 46 losers in 46 matches.

2^5 is 32, and 2^6 is 64, 47 being above 32 but below 65, we need 6 rounds.

Using Logic

Round	Matches	Remaining Players
1	15	32
2	16	16
3	8	8
4	4	4
5	2	2
6	1	1 (the winner)
Totals	6	46

Do you think that using mathematics i.e. powers is mind games or logic?

My view would be that deciding to use powers, and their application is logical, the mind games part is in realising that they are a possible approach, and challenging whether they are the best approach to the problem in hand. It is, however, very important not to allow yourself to get too concerned about such issues! What matters is finding an approach which works, not giving it a label. All the ideas and models used throughout the book should be used in such a manner.

1.2 ANAGRAMS

i.	E S T L B A E T N I N	TABLETENNIS
ii.	L W O R E P A O T	WATERPOLO
iii.	R L I S D B L I A	BILLIARDS
iv	N T O B M A I D N	BADMINTON
v.	K E O H Y C	HOCKEY
vi	T G I S R W E L N	WRESTLING
vii.	E C Q T O U R	CROQUET
viii.	R Y H A E C R	ARCHERY
ix.	E K C T I R C	CRICKET
x.	C A H E T I L T S	ATHLETICS
xi.	A D Y S E W P E	SPEEDWAY
xii.	N O H I S T O G	SHOOTING
xiii.	K B L A T L B E S	BASKETBALL
xiv.	I L U N C G R	CURLING
xv.	K I Y D L D T S W N I	TIDDLYWINKS
xvi.	R C O S L S E A	LACROSSE
xvii.	E D I S O M N O	DOMINOES
xviii.	M G S I W N I M	SWIMMING
xix	G A R H D U S T	DRAUGHTS
xx.	G N Y C I L C	CYCLING

This question was aimed at developing your mind games skills, further examples being provided throughout this book and in the companion Mind Management one.

Yes, I know xiii is wrong. One of the A's was missed out in the question! I hope you didn't spend too long looking for the answer, but if you did spend a long time on it, you should question whether you are too much of a perfectionist! Mistakes happen in real life: when should you decide to 'call it a day' and accept that you can't work out one of the 'answers'?!

This is a very difficult lesson to learn, and the answer clearly depends on how important getting it right is. So as to avoid discouraging you from making good attempts at future questions, I assure you that no further 'deliberate mistakes' are made.

1.3 GETTING RESULTS
Telephone, fax, courier or e-mail!

Hopefully you at least considered such methods, but it is worrying how often we can become blind to other approaches / ideas if certain ones have been put into our minds, or are habitually used. If your immediate reaction to seeing the suggested methods was 'that's not fair, they weren't mentioned as possibilities', you really do need to flex your mind.

Are such methods available in this case? If so, are they sufficiently secure / reliable for this information? The results may already be on the computer system, and the Head of School able to access them herself! Fax may not be either reliable or secure enough, and a telephone call could be quite time consuming (though not as much as a return journey) and open to mistakes when reading out names and results.

Consideration should be given to the purpose of the information. It is required for 'an important meeting', but would it matter if one or two results were wrong? Is she actually more interested in the total number of passes?

If the above methods are not feasible, you may have to go yourself, or get someone else to take them. It may well be the case that someone else from your site is attending the meeting or going to the other campus for another reason. Being as important as you are, you may decide your own time is too valuable, and send one of your minions!

As is usually the case in real life, the information supplied is not really sufficient for making definitely the best decision, and the one chosen will depend on the assumptions made. These should include the latest acceptable time for delivery of the results, the consequences of late or non-delivery, and whether you are willing / available to stay overnight to be absolutely certain of on-time delivery in person. The Head of School has requested the results by 8.00am, but is that the real deadline? Does she really need them before that, so as to have time to read and think about them prior to the meeting? Would it be possible to delay use of the results until a late stage of the meeting, allowing later delivery? What time is the meeting?

It may be possible to clarify some of the uncertainties by discussing the situation with the Head of School, if available.

Some options could be eliminated e.g. coach on Wednesday morning other than the first one, but even catching that one might be risky — how reliable is the service at that time of day?

In practice, and assuming the simple solutions (telephone, fax, courier or e-mail) to not be available or suitable, most people would opt to go by car, probably due to such other unmentioned factors as convenience, flexibility, habit, laziness and fear of getting wet if it rained.

Chapter 2
Problem Solving

The problem is all inside your head, she said to me
The answer is easy if you take it logically
I'd like to help you in your struggle to be free
There must be fifty ways to leave your lover

Fifty Ways To Leave Your Lover
Paul Simon

There are 2 types of people in the world, those who put everything into 2 types...
And those who don't!

I have already shown a tendency towards the former, with the logical and mind games approaches outlined in chapter 1, but to prove I am actually the latter, I will consider three types of decision which are suitable for a logical approach:

>Problem Solving
>Decision Making
>Risk Management

Problem solving is viewed as the whole process from appreciating that there is a problem, through solving it, to learning from it. The other two focus on particular elements, with decision making looking at ways in which choice can be made between various possible solutions. Risk management deals with identification and consideration of the likelihood of particular problems arising and ways of lessening their consequences.

This chapter covers problem solving, with the next 2 chapters considering decision making and risk management respectively.

Problem Solving

In any situation there is a desired state. Problems arise when this desired state does not exist. For example, a continuous heartbeat is a desired state, if it stops beating: problem!

Control systems exist with the purpose of achieving such a desired state, or goal. A basic model for such a system is shown in diagram 2.1.

Diagram 2.1: A Basic Control System

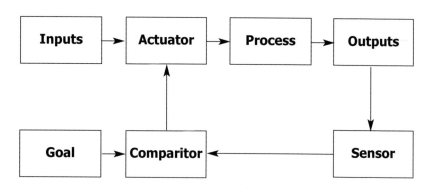

To explain the diagram consider a central heating system. Inputs to the system include the energy used by the boiler and the effects of the atmosphere. An actuator turns the boiler on and the process takes place, resulting in output of heat from the radiators. If there were no control on the system, the boiler would continue working and air temperature would rise to an uncomfortable level, with the boiler ultimately springing a leak or exploding.

In order to operate the control we need a sensor to measure the air temperature, feeding the information to a comparitor. This compares the actual temperature to the desired state or goal, in this case a pre-determined temperature, and signals to an actuator to turn the boiler off if the actual temperature is above target, and on if actual is below target. The whole process keeps repeating itself for as long as the system is switched on.

The above would be an extremely simple situation. In practice, it may be desirable to avoid constant switching on and off of the boiler, and several rooms may be covered by the same heating system, with different temperatures desired in different rooms. There may be a delay between the desired temperature being reached in the room(s) covered by the system and the sensor registering it. Such problems can be dealt with by such measures as careful location of the sensor, having additional sensors, additional radiators, and having a higher control temperature for switching the boiler off than for switching it on.

Another well known illustration of this type of system is the way in which we regulate our body temperature. Heat is generated as we digest our food, and carry out activities such as playing sport or thinking, and our bodies have a narrow optimum operating temperature range. The amount of heat required to keep our bodies within that range depends on the temperature of the surrounding air / water, allowing for any wind chill factor. There is often an imbalance between the heat automatically generated and that required, so our bodies have to take actions to restore equilibrium.

When too little heat is being generated, we either reduce the heat we are losing (put on more clothing, turn up the central heating boiler – see above! - move to a more sheltered spot – ideally the Bahamas!) or increase the amount we are generating (more exercise, eating more or shivering).

Too much heat generation requires us to increase the amount being lost to the atmosphere (perspire, which has a cooling effect as it evaporates, less clothing, increase the wind chill factor by using a fan, spread out our arms and legs) or decrease the amount we generate (relax, take it easy, eat less).

ASK SIR L

I want to consider means by which problems can be examined and, hopefully, put right. A seven stage process can be used: when you have a problem: ASK SIR L.

A ppreciate	a problem exists
S pecify	exactly what is / is not going wrong
K auses	of these events
S olutions	to return to the desired state
I mplementation	of the chosen solution
R eview	to check the solution is working
L earn	from the experience

(OK, I know causes starts with a curly c, not a kicking k, But ASC SIR L just isn't the same!)

Sir L also refers to the chivalrous knight, Lancelot, who will be demonstrating use of this process to us. Sir Lancelot was, you will recall, King Arthur's one true faithful servant (or am I getting confused with an old joke?)

It will be seen that the first 2 stages (appreciate and specify) equate to the sensor and comparitor in the basic control system shown in diagram 2.1, and the fifth (implement) to the actuator and process. That diagram did not include the identification of causes or generation of solutions stages, but a more complex version could have, as shown in diagram 2.2. Review of the effectiveness of the solution would be when the objectives and outputs were next compared, but learning from the experience would involve a conscious attempt to see that such problems were avoided in future.

Diagram 2.2: Control System: More Complex Showing Relationship to ASK SIR L Stages in Problem Solving

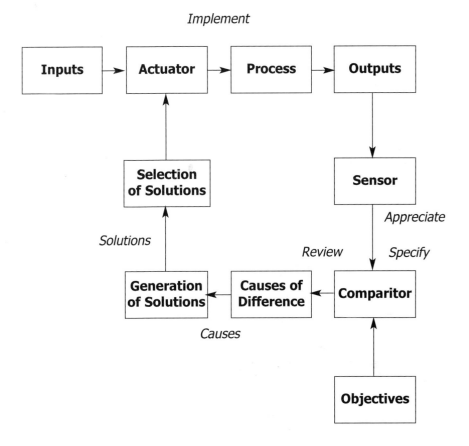

This logical systematic approach helps to ensure all facets of a problem are considered in a careful methodical manner. It can be used to practice emergency procedures so that the "correct" action to take in given situations can be determined, agreed and perfected in advance without the pressures and constraints faced when the event takes place. Karate experts practice routines so that they will automatically do the right thing if attacked by a 29 stone gorilla with a knife, while hospitals and the emergency services practice disaster scenarios such as road accidents or the receipt and treatment of war wounded. Cities in earthquake or hurricane zones have established escape routes.

The approach can also be usefully applied to common problem areas by development of Expert Systems. A panel of experts compiles a guide to tackling particular problems for use by anyone able to follow the instructions correctly. A well-known example is compilation of diagnosis procedures by specialists in rare illnesses, which can then be used by all doctors. One which I can personally vouch for is in the New Book of the Road published by the AA/Reader's Digest: "A step-by-step guide to help a stranded motorist to find and correct a fault and get himself home". But how can you get your hands on a pair of tights (for use as an emergency fan belt, of course) when you need to?

In recent years, numerous disasters have taken place (e.g. Concorde plane crash, Hatfield train crash, death of Princess Diana, loss of Russian submarine). The logical systematic approach under discussion is ideally suited for analysing their causes and hopefully preventing their recurrence. It is illustrated below, however, by examination of what could be the biggest disaster ever to face humanity: global warming.

Problem Solving

This was chosen partly because it is such an interesting, unresolved problem, but also because you will doubtless have thought about it to some extent, which will help you see how the points made relate to the general model. It would be very good practice if, having read the relevant explanation, you thought about how each stage related to global warming before reading my views.

In addition, I would not want to give the impression that problem solving is always easy. Consideration of a real life issue will hopefully illustrate some of the difficulties involved in using any model, and solving any complicated, difficult problem. It is important to recognise from the outset that models are simplifications of the real world, so do not reflect its intricacies. They should be applied to particular situations intelligently and thoughtfully.

So......ASK SIR L

A ppreciate   a problem exists
S pecify   exactly what is / is not going wrong
K auses   of these events

S olutions   to return to the desired state
I mplementation of the chosen solution
R eview   to check the solution is working

L earn   from the experience

First Stage in Decision Making

Appreciate
This is the first stage in the model, aimed at recognising that a problem exists. It is extremely important, since failure to do so early enough can mean there is insufficient time to deal with the problem when it is identified. Many organisations carry out internal analyses to ensure their systems, processes and resources are sound, and environmental scanning to identify possible external problems. This is often summarised as a SWOT analysis, examining internal Strengths and Weaknesses, and external Opportunities and Threats. The problem is producing a strategy which uses strengths in areas of opportunity to achieve objectives. (As will be shown in chapter 3, it is also important not to just ignore weaknesses and threats! They should either be tackled or avoided).

Strategic analysis is a major topic of extreme importance, and if faced with carrying one out you should read several books on the subject. No, not now. Finish this one first!

Each time you see the following illustration, you should attempt to relate the part of the ASK SIR L model under discussion to the global warming problem. Whether you do so in a pub is optional!

Problem Solving

So how should the global warming problem have been appreciated?

In the case of global warming, individuals made casual observations along the lines of 'the summers seem to be hotter and last longer than I remember' or 'it doesn't seem to snow in the winter anymore'. My wife blames me for the incessant rain we have suffered ever since I made the observation that 'there is no need to take an umbrella any more: it hardly ever rains'.

The first real concern came, however, from geophysicists claiming to have identified a genuine upward trend in world temperatures. The problem is in determining whether or not this claim is valid.

A fundamental question is, what is the normal temperature of the Earth? Clearly, different locations will have different temperatures, and they will vary depending on time of day, season, and possibly long-term cycles. We must decide which locations to use and establish ways of measuring their temperature and establishing any long-term trend.

Scientists and the organisations they work for are extremely keen to make important breakthroughs and discoveries for all sorts of reasons (reputation / fame / attract funding / thirst for knowledge / thrill of discovery etc.) Their claims could be false, due to deliberate falsification or manipulation of evidence, faulty analysis, invalid conclusions, and so on. They must, consequently, be treated with caution and subjected to rigorous investigation, carried out by other scientists and organisations often, for example in the field of medicine, under Government control. Papers are published in influential journals, conferences and symposia held, and general debate ensues.

In many cases the claim cannot easily be proved or disproved. Even in these days of information technology and international travel, the Earth is still fairly large so if trying to determine whether global warming is taking place it is not a case of just saying "put this thermometer under your tongue" and then reading the result. The Earth does not have a mouth or equivalent orifice!

Specify

In this stage we want to identify exactly what the problem is. What is going wrong and, often of equal importance when it comes to identifying causes and generating solutions, what is NOT going wrong. In order to do this, it is necessary to establish as many facts about the problem as possible, and experimentation may be required.

It can be useful to think about the 6 classic questions: Who, What, Where, When, How and Why? This is the deductive approach to problem solving, the hope being that by identifying the problem exactly, the cause and solution will become obvious. Conan Doyle's character Sherlock Holmes was the supposed arch exponent of this technique, being able to tell which type of school a teacher victim had taught at: "Elementary, my dear Watson"! (OK, I admit to feeling ashamed of that one. I promise the jokes won't get any worse - well, not much worse. Probably.)

Often, particularly when considering how and why the problem occurs, attempts to specify the problem in this way will move into the area of causes, which is the next stage in the model. This is fine, providing the solver does not move on completely until the specification stage has been properly carried out. The whole process is iterative. Facts may be identified in the specification stage which suggest certain causes, leading to a search for more facts to assist in verifying whether or not those suggested are the actual causes.

Taking the 6 classic questions in turn:

Who is affected by the problem? Certain individuals or types? Are any individuals / types not affected? Discovery of small pox vaccine followed realisation that milkmaids rarely suffered from the disease.

What happens / does not happen? Is there anything which might be expected to happen, but does not? Your radio does not switch on - try the kettle in the same socket: it works, so the fault must be with the radio, lead or its plug; does it work with batteries?...

Where does it happen? Is there anywhere that the particular problem does not happen? You suffer from mouth ulcers, but they went when you were on holiday in Greece. Experiment by taking some more holidays, to other countries, or by having time off work but staying at home. This may help identify whether the ulcers are caused by work, something in your home environment, something you eat...

When does it happen? Are there any times when it does not happen? Many criminals have been caught because they carried out their crimes on Thursday afternoons, or because the firm's takings increased dramatically when they went on holiday!

How does it happen? What is the underlying process? Is there a chain of events which all have to occur before the problem takes place? Does it happen suddenly, quickly, explosively, noisily...? Does it always take place in the same way? Are there any ways or circumstances in which it never happens?

The underlying logic behind a suggested cause of a problem can often be tested in this way: exactly how would the problem result? The Paddington train crash occurred when two trains approached each other on the same track and collided. How did it happen? Same track used for both directions; train passed through a red signal; driver unclear as to which signal referred to his track; too many signals; no 'fail safe' mechanism to prevent passing a red signal or to stop the trains before they hit...

Why does it happen? When it does not happen, what is different? This is clearly leading into the cause stage, which is aimed at bringing together all the facts about the problem and identifying exactly what causes it. Before going on to that, however, I will carry out the specification stage for the global warming problem. Don't forget to spend some time thinking about it before reading my views.

Collect your thoughts...

Problem Solving

Despite concerns having been expressed and research undertaken for a number of years, many people still do not accept that global warming is taking place at all. This highlights the difficulty faced in attempting to specify exactly what is happening.

It is patently true that some parts of the Earth have been hotter than usual in recent years, but that might be perfectly normal: other parts have, no doubt, been colder than usual. (Russian ships were able to travel to the North Pole in open water during summer 2000, which does make it seem that something unusual is taking place).

Aspects of 'global warming' we might be concerned with would include:
- has the overall climate changed, if so, to what extent and how fast?
- is there a continuing trend?
- does it apply uniformly around the Earth or is it concentrated in particular locations?
- is the temperature of the water/air/land rising fastest?
- are the polar ice- caps melting?
- are any other events occurring that could be linked to this problem e.g. unusual weather patterns or increased levels of pollution?

To answer such queries, readings must be taken for several years at thousands of locations. Thermal photographs can be taken of certain areas, or of the whole Earth's surface from space. Air temperatures are known to fluctuate wildly, so some measurements may be better taken deep in the oceans, high in the stratosphere, or inside the Earth's crust - the problem then being that any change that is occurring could take years to reach those locations anyway. Models and computer simulations have been prepared in an attempt to pull together the results and draw conclusions.

As part of the appreciate / specify stages, it is important to decide how large the problem is / could be as this will indicate the amount of effort which should be put into solving it. In the case of global warming, we are concerned with its potential effects on the environment. These are far from clear, but could be extreme and likely to require fast, drastic actions. Various predictions have been made as to the effect of, say, a 3-degree Celsius rise in global temperature:

- if the ice-caps melt, there would be a rise in the height of the oceans of several metres; much of southern England would be submerged;
- many areas currently ideal for growing crops would turn into desert, including the American grain belt;
- Northern Europe's climate would become Mediterranean;
- I would have to take up mountain walking instead of skiing!

I would have to take up mountain walking

■ general change might occur in weather patterns - is it coincidence that so many major storms have hit the UK in recent years?

The likely accuracy of such predictions can only be guessed at, but there does seem a tendency for Doomsday Scenarios to be produced, for the reasons mentioned previously. Economists and weather forecasters have similar models for predicting the future and their accuracy is legendary! It has been suggested, however, that in the last Ice Age (you remember-the one where ice several thousand feet thick came down to about Birmingham) the global temperature was only about 2 degrees centigrade below what it is now, so some fairly spectacular changes can be relied on if it does increase by 3 degrees!

The counter argument is that, if global warming is not occurring or is just part of a natural cycle, any action taken will be a waste at best, and at worst could create a problem where one did not exist.

Is the variation normal / acceptable / desirable? In the case of heartbeats, considerable variation is normal depending on level of activity / time of day / temperature / when you last ate / what you are wearing etc.. This is highly desirable as it is part of the body's control system, attempts to prevent or correct it could prove fatal. (This does not of course mean that all variations in heartbeat are welcomed!)

Analysis tells us that variations in global temperature have occurred cyclically throughout history. Major ice ages have lasted thousands of years before returning to what we think is normal. Mini ice ages of a few hundred years have seen relatively cold periods come and go, while much credence is given to a theory that smaller fluctuation cycles of about 11 years also occur, possibly linked to a cycle in the number of sunspots. Is the current rise (if it exists) part of one of these cycles, and if so, could we stop it even if we tried, and if we did, could that result in unforeseen reactions sending us into all kinds of terrible climate changes? Perhaps the Earth has a natural rhythm, possibly deliberately placed there by nature / God to ensure survival of the fittest or wipe out species that get too clever and endanger the whole planet?! Can we play God?

More generally, this can be thought of as deciding whether a particular problem is ours to solve. There is a fine balance between

not allowing yourself to become involved in issues that are best left to others, while ensuring you are not ducking legitimate responsibilities.

In the case of global warming, it might be tempting to think it is too big a problem for individuals to solve, so should be left to governments, or God. The danger here is that such an approach may, if we all adopt it, result in us individually acting in such a manner as to collectively worsen the problem.

My opinion is that we should only attempt to alter the climate if it can be shown that:
- there is a high likelihood that global warming is occurring;
- to such an extent that it may threaten our continued comfortable existence; and
- such warming is not due to natural fluctuations or events, but is in fact being caused by our interference.

This leads on to the next stage in the model, causes, but also illustrates how, in practice, the stages tend to overlap.

Causes

This stage attempts to identify what is causing the specified problem to occur. It is important to distinguish between cause and effect, so that when we come to look for solutions, we do not mistakenly attempt to treat symptoms instead of the underlying causes. Note the use of the word 'mistakenly': it is often, including many health problems, not possible to stop the causes, and we have to fall back on dealing with the effects.

In complicated situations, the cause may not be immediately apparent, so a good deal of analysis and thought may be required in order to establish what it is. It can be useful to break this down into three elements:

Potential causes	- of this type of problem
Possible causes	- of this particular problem
Actual causes	- in this case

Potential Causes
Time to think!

This is the part most people skip, going instead for the most obvious cause and often getting it completely wrong. What should happen is a genuine attempt to consider all events or circumstances that could result in a situation like that under consideration. An effective and commonly used approach is 'brain storming' in which you list all the potential causes you can think of, including those you might be tempted to reject out of hand. This is best done in a group, so that individuals spin ideas off of each other. Chapter 6 examines the importance of, and issues surrounding, problem solving in groups.

Turning to our problem: What could cause the Earth's temperature to rise? My thoughts follow, but before reading on, have you any ideas of your own?

A: Increased heat
1. from within
2. from outside
3. generated on the surface

B: Less heat
1. escaping
2. being tied up

C: Your ideas!

Taking these in turn:

A: Increased Heat

1. From Within
I can see 3 possibilities (can you see others?):

i) A change has taken place in the processes within the Earth's core, such as the commencement of nuclear fission or fusion.
ii) Very hot material from near the centre has started to come nearer the surface.
iii) More heat is escaping from vents in the Earth's crust (e.g. volcanoes/hot springs etc.)
iv) Any ideas?

2. From Outside

i) The sun is giving off more heat.
ii) We have moved closer to the sun.
iii) Less heat lost on route between the sun and earth.
iv) Another source of external heat has occurred (I haven't noticed 2 sunrises everyday, but for example, could there be more matter in space such as interstellar gas causing increased friction, and hence warming, as we pass through it?)
v) Some (invisible) barrier that was protecting the Earth from excessive heat has weakened or disappeared. In the opinion of most scientists, this is the major cause. The ozone layer (which performs that function) has been greatly reduced, with reports that the hole in the ozone layer above the Antarctic is now 3 times bigger than the United States. It is important to consider whether this would have been considered as a potential cause if it hadn't been stumbled on independently by researchers measuring the ozone layer's thickness. If you thought some of the other ideas were ludicrous, wouldn't this one have seemed equally unlikely if you hadn't already heard about it?
vi) Any ideas?

3. Generated On The Surface
i) Natural causes (I can't think of any).
ii) More people. The world population is growing rapidly. Could the increase in such things as domestic fires have a significant effect?
iii) Changing way of life. Does the fact that a higher percentage of people use fridges, cars, planes etc. matter?
iv) Increased industrialisation. Heat from industrial processes, including the burning of vast areas of forest to clear land.
v) Any ideas?

B: Less Heat
1. Escaping
i) Different types of material reflect heat with different degrees of efficiency. Has there been a change in the make-up of the Earth's surface resulting in less heat being reflected?
ii) Is the heat being retained on the surface instead of attempting to leave the Earth's atmosphere?
iii) The famous Greenhouse Effect. Is a barrier developing that is preventing heat from escaping the Earth's atmosphere?
iv) Any ideas?

2. Tied Up

i) Energy cannot be created or used up, it just changes form. Throughout history, energy from the sun has been stored in the form of coal / oil etc.. In recent years, we have been freeing this energy by burning these resources. This is closely linked to 'increased heat generated on the surface' but is a different angle on the problem. In fact, a possibility if warming does take place is that methane gas, currently frozen under the tundra, warms up and escapes into the atmosphere, worsening the greenhouse effect further.

ii) Any ideas?

C: Any Other Ideas?

Possible / Actual Causes

Having identified as many potential causes as possible, it is necessary to eliminate any that clearly do not apply in this case so as to leave only those possible causes of the problem faced. If carrying out this analysis in practice, one would then carry out research, analysis and investigation with the objective of establishing the actual cause(s).

The following table considers the potential causes identified above, and weights them according to their likely actual importance, in my opinion. I have had to adopt this kind of approach because I cannot definitely eliminate particular potential causes, the weakness being that the weightings are very subjective and could affect the results considerably. What weightings would you have used?

Description	Comments	Weight (%)
A Increased Heat		
1) from within		
i) Change in Processes	Extremely unlikely. Why should there be such a change?	0
ii) Hot material rising	No scientific evidence, but could be a cause	2
iii) More volcanoes	Possible contributor but low importance here. More likely effect under **B**)i).	2
iv) Any ideas?		0
2) from outside		
i) Sun hotter	Many scientists believe the energy released by the sun varies in 11 year cycles, linked to sun spot activity. Could be a temporary cause.	4
ii) Sun closer	Extremely unlikely. I assume scientists measure this easily / accurately and they haven't mentioned it!	0
iii) Less lost en route	Extremely unlikely, for the same reason.	0
iv) External source	Extremely unlikely.	2
v) Weakened barrier	Ozone layer: the mint with the hole. As discussed previously, this is an accepted major cause of global warming	32
vi) Your ideas		0
3) Generated on the Surface		
i) Natural causes		2
ii) More people	Generally accepted that this has more effect on **A**)2)v) through carbon dioxide and CFCs (used in fridges / aerosols) attacking the ozone layer, and on **B**)1)iii)	6
iii) Lifestyle		8
iv) Industry / Deforestatiov)	Main effect on **B**)1)iii)	6
Your ideas		0
		39

Description	Comments	Weight (%)
B Less heat		
1) escaping		
i) Less reflection	Smoke and other pollutants in the atmosphere tend to reflect heat badly. Smaller polar ice-caps, which are good reflectors	12
ii) Retained on surface	Hard to see a major change (other than the possible warming which is the problem under consideration).	0
iii) Barrier	Smoke and pollutants again. Ironically, a high percentage of energy arrives from the sun in a form which is reflected by the ozone layer but is unaffected by the pollution barrier. It then changes to a form which is affected by the pollution barriers, so it can't get back out! The fear is that the ozone layer is disappearing while the pollution barrier is increasing. More heat getting in combined with less getting out!	12
iv) Your ideas		0
2) Tied up		
i) Depleting Resources	Energy is tied up in natural resources such as coal. If we use these up faster than they are replaced, the energy is released, often in the form of heat.	2
ii) Your ideas		0
C) I have left 10% of the weighting for all ideas you may have!		10
Total		**100**

Overall, it can be seen that, in my view, the underlying causes of any global warming that is taking place are the smoke and pollution generated by industrial activities, deforestation and vehicle exhaust fumes, and the use of CFCs, all of which contribute to weakening of the ozone layer. I may have allowed myself to be put off considering some potential causes properly since it would be apparently impossible to stop them. This would be a very bad mistake since other people might see ways in which they could be stopped, other actions might be possible to cope with the situation, and it might make me blame something else, which in fact is not the cause.

Solutions

Having appreciated that we have a problem, specified its precise nature and scope, and identified its causes, we now need to consider how to solve it. This can be divided into two aspects, generation of possible solutions and selection of the solution to be implemented.

Generation

Suitable solutions will depend upon the problem being tackled. The following discussion covers a wide range of approaches and ideas, but must not be assumed to include every aspect relevant to every problem. As with all other sections of this book, it must be used intelligently and thoughtfully.

Ideally, we are looking for solutions which will directly tackle the causes of the problem. If this is not possible, we may have to deal with the effects and symptoms instead. Many medical treatments are palliative, not curative, the most obvious example being that for the common cold - no cure has been found for the actual complaint, but any number of products are available to relieve the symptoms.

We want solutions which really will solve the problem / achieve our objectives. There is a danger of accepting a solution as valid without properly testing to ensure it will work in all practical circumstances. The head-long rush towards internet solutions for every problem known to man is a good illustration of this point.

Internet shopping has been heralded as the next great break-through, but in practice is not being taken up to anything like the extent originally predicted. It does seem to be popular for purchase of very standard, well known products and services (theatre tickets, insurance) but less so for those where purchasers want some personal service or advice (holidays) or want to see the product before buying (clothing). Many people have tried it and found it to be very similar to catalogue shopping, so use it for similar purchases.

Internet shopping does not provide some of the other elements found in traditional approaches, such as socialising, but it may be more convenient, particularly in bad weather or for less mobile or particularly busy individuals. It is used more by men than women, which may be an important factor since women generally shop more than men.

A particular difficulty which was frequently not given proper consideration when adopting this approach has been delivery of the product to the customer. Various solutions have been tried including post, white vans and customer pick-up.

Returning to more general considerations, it is important that we consider a wide range of solutions so as to ensure we include the best. The brainstorming technique previously mentioned can be very useful here: all possible solutions or part solutions, regardless of whether they seem at all valid at first sight, are listed and considered. Attempts are made to spin ideas off of each solution to see whether new ones can be generated, or combinations of ideas made.

The idea of using combinations of ideas is an important one. Very often a solution 'package' will be far more effective than any individual solution, and care should be taken to continue searching for improvements to particular proposals. Minor (or major) adaptations could result in greater likelihood of success or improved outcomes.

In some cases, analysis of the problem will have revealed that it resulted from a chain of events rather than one specific cause. Solutions here may revolve around ensuring that a particular link in the chain cannot occur again. Security of information is now a big problem for many organisations aware of the possibility of industrial espionage or malicious damage by computer hackers or computer viruses. Restrictions on physical access can be used, but

Problem Solving

remote access is often available and necessary for their staff to properly carry out their tasks. Passwords can be used but many people forget them, write them down next to the keypad, or use something obvious like their car's number plate. In the words of Ann Robinson: "You are the weakest link". A determined hacker can often find a way through.

To avoid this, the organisations set up 'fire walls' in their systems designed to detect any potential threats to the system from incoming communications, and prevent them gaining access. Whatever means of attack are deployed by the 'invaders', whatever links there are in their chain, the fire wall will prevent damage. Of course, the invaders will look for holes in the wall, and so the game goes on.

The concept of strategic analysis was mentioned earlier in this chapter as a major topic of extreme importance, with the advice that if faced with carrying one out you should read several books on the subject. The basic problem was stated as the need to produce a strategy which uses strengths in areas of opportunity to achieve objectives. This is clearly relevant to solution generation, and I will just mention a few aspects which need consideration:

Porter's 5 Forces (suppliers, buyers, substitute products, new entrants, and existing competitors); TQM (total quality management); focus on customers; 'Lean' organisations and 'just in time' philosophy; PESTLED (political, economic, societal, technological, legal, ecological, demographic) analysis of the external environment; 'green' moral and ethical issues; financial and operational gearing; product portfolio; product life cycle; Boston Matrix (market share and potential growth); product range; loss leaders; marketing mix (product, place, price, promotion were the original '4P's', but others are sometimes added e.g. people, profit); Porter's 3 generic strategies (cost leadership, differentiation, specialisation); market penetration or skimming; Ansoff's Matrix (new or old products, in new or old markets); Kaplan and Norton's Balanced Scorecard; added value; Porter's value chains; business process re-engineering.

I hope that has convinced you of the need to read that book.

When the problem we are dealing with is one of trying to avoid serious adverse events in the future, solutions are likely to revolve around lessening the likelihood of the event occurring, and minimising its effects and consequences if it does occur. This kind of problem is covered in chapter 4: Risk Management.

Selection

Once a wide range of possible solutions has been generated, a decision must be made as to which one, or package, to implement. For straight-forward problems, just listing the points for and against each solution may reveal the most beneficial one.

In complex decisions, it will be necessary to establish and analyse the relative merits of each option. Very often, there may be a range of factors to be borne in mind, e.g. cost, speed, certainty and quality, and it may be necessary to trade-off advantages and disadvantages associated with particular options. Some kind of a decision making model will have to be established, a commonly used approach being to weight each factor for its importance, then score each solution package as to how well it achieves each factor. Multiplying the scores by the factor weightings will enable an overall score for each solution to be established. Decision making techniques are covered in more detail in the next chapter.

Selection: How not to do it!

Solutions must be fair, equitable and acceptable to all affected parties. However the eventual decision is taken, the 'down side' must be considered. Are there any people adversely affected by it? Can it be adapted to remove or minimise such adverse aspects? Can those individuals be compensated? This is considered further in the implementation section below, and in chapter 6 (Groups).

Over-reaction to the problem should be avoided since that could cause new problems far worse than the original. In the modern media-driven world, there is always a danger that a particular event will be blown-up out of proportion, and the decision maker must beware being swept up in the ensuing mayhem and hysteria. An illustration of this is the events which followed the death of Princess Diana. During the immediate aftermath, many commentators were claiming that it would be the end of the Royal family, while others wanted all paparazzi shot at dawn. In practice, after a few weeks, everything was back to normal, with celebrities hassled as much as ever.

Avoiding over-reaction is an important consideration in the political arena. It seems to be an assumed part of the role of the opposition to demand a public enquiry followed by drastic action whenever a bad event occurs, and a common tactic adopted by the government is setting up a committee to report on the matter. By the time it does so, the heat has gone out of the situation, and a far more rational decision can be taken.

Getting the timing right is a very important part of decision making. Early decisions facilitate speedy resolution of the problem, but there are often good reasons for delay. There is a clear trade-off between possibly making an ill-informed decision, and constantly putting off decisions waiting for better information.

It takes time to obtain and analyse all relevant facts, generate solutions and decide which to adopt. It is also often possible to remove some of the uncertainties surrounding particular solutions by trials, models or simulations, all of which take time.

Trials could be temporary adoption of the proposed solution for the whole organisation, in particular locations, or on volunteers. New products are very often tested on focus groups or launched in one part of the country. Changes to the rules of sports are often tried out in a particular competition, in minor leagues, in friendlies, or for one season. Models and simulations can be numerical, using mathematical formulae, or more in line with the traditional use of the word, a physical model of say, a new component or office layout.

Turning back to the global warming illustration, the causes identified earlier are increasingly being accepted as valid, and several steps suggested, and taken, to deal with them. These include lessening the use of CFCs in aerosols and lead in petrol - a problem being that the products used to replace them are suspected by some scientists of having as bad effects as the ones they are replacing! Diesel was promoted as a cleaner alternative to petrol, and taxed at a lower rate to encourage motorists to switch, until subsequent analysis revealed that it is at least as bad a pollutant as petrol.

Some feeble attempts have been made to reduce the use of vehicles by encouraging people to walk, cycle or car share, but investment in public transport has been poor. International air travel is the fastest-growing and most polluting form of transport, yet governments have so far exempted it from global warming measures.

An interesting definition problem comes into discussion of lessening use of CFCs. Their use is actually still increasing, but not as fast as it would have if attempts weren't being made to restrict their use, so many politicians claim that use has lessened!! i.e. from what it would have been, not from what it was!

The fact that little real action is being taken to genuinely reduce use of pollutants is particularly concerning since their effects are not immediate. Many scientists believe CFCs take up to 10 years to move up to the ozone layer and attack it, other pollutants taking up to 100 years to do their damage, e.g. having been buried in a refuse tip, working their way through the soil and into rivers etc.. Three points result:

- returning to the year 2000 level of use by 2010 implies CFC damage at above year 2000 levels until 2020.
- damage done up to year 2000 results from CFC usage up to 1990. Production levels back then were far below current levels.
- 10+ years is beyond many people's event horizons. They are not prepared to change their habits (e.g. walk or cycle instead of driving) or give up their jobs as car workers now, to stop possible / unproven bad effects many years hence.

Many firms now plant replacement trees whenever they chop one down, greater recycling is being encouraged, and a general move against the 'throw away society' mentality is developing.

It may be fair to conclude that individuals are becoming increasingly persuaded that action is required, are aware of what that action must be, and are really just waiting for central leadership and action. Governments, particularly Western ones, seem to be unwilling to take the necessary steps, however, presumably more concerned about the threat of short-term unpopularity than long-term disaster.

When deciding which solution package to adopt, it is important to check that, if correctly implemented, it will solve the problem. A danger can be going too far, and that could apply here - we don't want to end up in an ice age!

These are clearly implementation issues, and lead towards the next step in the model.

Implementation

Many people think, often subconsciously, that once they have identified the right solution package their job is done: they had a problem, and now they have solved it! Unfortunately, this is not the case, and very often the hard work is just beginning. A problem is not dealt with until the solution has been implemented and reviewed to ensure it has worked. Even then, an important element remains: to learn from the whole process. In this section, I am focusing on implementation.

Possibly the most important part of implementation is to get started (well, why don't you then?!)

Bite the bullet! Don't put off implementing 'nasty' or important solutions, since this will only delay achievement of a successful outcome, and the knowledge that you still have the task to do will be bad psychologically. Where the solution requires a great deal of effort, it is often difficult to know where to start: how do you eat an elephant?

A good approach here is to start with some easy areas in which you are confident of success. This helps you feel you are making progress, and gain credibility with any other people involved, eliciting their commitment and enthusiasm. As confidence and experience grow, other parts of the solution should become easier, such that ultimately only a few difficult areas should remain. This technique is sometimes called the 'Swiss cheese approach', referring to that type of cheese which has holes throughout: at the start, the solution looks like a solid, unmanageable lump, but each bite size chunk dealt with is another hole in the cheese. Suddenly, there isn't much cheese left to eat. How do you eat an elephant? One bite at a time!

Project Management
This term refers to the planning and execution of complicated solutions, within a framework of time and budgetary constraints. Considerable thought and analysis is required to establish how and when each element of the solution will be implemented, with key result areas and milestones established so that progress towards a successful solution can be monitored.

Often, certain elements of a problem will have to be completed before others can start, so plans will have to include details of their inter-relationships. These can be plotted as a network, showing exactly which activities have to be completed before others can start. Critical paths can be established, showing those activities which must be completed on time if the whole project is to run smoothly.

While it is desirable psychologically to have great faith in positive completion of the plan, it is equally important to consider the possibility that things may go wrong. Possible bail-out and cut-off points should be considered, and ultimate fall back positions established. Ideally, the plan should be such that partial completion will at least achieve some of the objectives, but this cannot always be done: when the channel tunnel was under construction, the builders kept running out of money and going back to the financiers for more. They were then faced with the choice of losing all the money they had invested to date and ending up with half a tunnel, or putting more in and hopefully getting a whole hole. On each occasion, the right decision seemed to be pour more money in, but the cost ultimately rose from an original £4.6 billion to around £11 billion.

When major changes are taking place, and because implementation is so complex and crucial for success, some organisations use specialist transformation experts. My view is that, since change is so prevalent in modern society and organisations, transformation skills are a vital need of all modern managers. Each time the skills are bought in, internal managers are denied the opportunity to develop them, resulting in a cycle of incompetent internal management being supported by expensive consultants. Change Management is the most important element of any manager's role, and it can be argued that anything not involving change is really just administration. (Bring on the Masters of Business Administration!)

Dealing with people is a crucial part of change management, and is now considered in some detail.

Force Field Analysis
Refers to consideration of the forces which exist for and against successful implementation, and their relative strengths. It derives from the basic laws of physics that for an object to be in a state of equilibrium, forces acting on it must be equal and opposite, and in order to move an object, a force must be applied to it sufficient to overcome any resistance.

Applying this to our situation, implementation of a change requires forces in favour sufficient to overcome any resistance. Forces in favour will include the effort being put in by those attempting implementation, level of support from senior management, and any general recognition of the need for change. Resistance will come from people adversely affected by the change, any general climate of mistrust, and any lack of required skills or facilities.

We need to make the positive forces stronger than the negative ones, and the remainder of this section considers means of doing so. Some of the suggestions made are very political and risky in that they could easily backfire: if people feel they are being manipulated, they are likely to become very hostile, and become a strong negative force.

Let the force be with you!

A useful starting point is to consider the attitude spectrum of those affected. This refers to the idea that people's attitudes can vary from being:

- a champion of the change - extremely keen to see its adoption;
- a disciple - not as proactive as a champion, but willing to spread the word;
- an acceptor - basically agreeing with the change, happy to go along with it, but not actually 'selling it' to others;
- a coper - not really bothered about it, tending to ignore it until it affects them, then doing the minimum to respond to it;
- unconcerned - not involved at all, possibly because they are unaware of the changes taking place, they do not feel affected by them, are otherwise engaged, or just not interested;
- a passive rejecter - basically against the change, but not sufficiently concerned to do anything against it (other than probably make adverse comments if the topic comes up);
- an active rejecter - sufficiently against the change to act to prevent its implementation. This may take relatively mild forms such as writing adverse reports and trying to mobilise resistance, but may go as far as to prepare and attempt to implement different plans, or even take deliberately hostile actions such as sabotage.

How can We Change the Overall Balance of Attitudes in Our Favour?

Firstly, we should recognise the fact that different people will have different levels of influence in the eventual decision, and concentrate our efforts on those with most influence. There are many types and sources of influence, including position, experience, past success (or failure), knowledge and skill relevant to the situation, contact networks, persuasive skills (written and verbal), charisma, and negative power i.e. the potential an individual or group has to interfere with the implementation of something they disagree with. Power and influence are discussed in more detail in chapter 6.

Next, we could attempt to change the group involved in the decision by seeking out potential influential allies and champions, persuading them of the validity and importance of our cause, and encouraging them to get involved. At the same time, we might try to remove some people from the group, possibly by encouraging them to get involved in other issues, or take a new post, either in this organisation or a different one!

We could attempt to move individuals or groups towards the top of the list, either one step at a time, or by complete conversion from rejection to champion in one move. The former is often easier to achieve, but the latter is more dramatic, satisfying, and has greater overall effect if achieved. Very often a person who has swapped sides becomes a very strong champion of their new position, a common example being how often ex-smokers are first to complain if someone 'lights up'. How can we change people's attitudes?

Communication is a vital aspect of influencing people, and is discussed in detail in chapter 6. Here, I will just mention the need to 'sell' the change to affected individuals. Explain the need for change and show, as far as possible, that it is their problem as well as yours - your change becomes our change. For example, if productivity has to be improved, explain to the relevant workers the consequences of failing to do so: redundancy.

Gain Commitment

Involve those affected by the change from the start. Consult them, encouraging contributions and participation in both planning and execution. Empathise with people, attempting to see the change from their viewpoint. What constraints and practicalities will they be faced with? Keep (and be seen to be) flexible, ready to look for a change which will help overcome their problems. Be willing to compromise and make deals so long as the basic problem will still be solved. There is a saying that a camel is a horse built by a committee, and there is clear danger in allowing too much compromise to result in a solution which meets no-one's objectives. Always remember, however, that a camel is ideally suited to its environment, so sometimes you should 'build a camel'.

Have you got time for a camel joke? (With vast apologies to anyone who knows anything about camels, for reasons which will become obvious no doubt).

Camelette: *Mum, why have I got these long eye-lashes?*
Mrs C: *To keep the desert sand out of your eye.*

Camelette: *Mum, why have I got these big flat feet?*
Mrs C: *To stop you sinking in the desert sand.*

Camelette: *Mum, why have I got this big hump on my back?*
Mrs C *For storing fat and water so you can go for days across the desert without eating or drinking.*

Camelette: *Mum, why do we live in London Zoo?*

I do know another camel joke, involving two bricks, but this is not the right time or place...

Look for common ground, emphasising the extent of agreement between you, thereby narrowing down the differences so that explanation can focus on them. Show how those affected will benefit or can minimise their losses.

Demonstrate the effectiveness of your intended solution by carrying out pilot schemes with people who are in favour of the change. If this is not possible, refer to previous successful implementations, possibly in other organisations. Show how well you have considered and planned the change, including discussion of any areas they are concerned about.

Encourage a positive attitude towards change: Change = Challenge = Growth, and do not undermine this attitude by carrying out changes in a deceitful, underhand manner. If people had bad experiences and felt exploited following previous changes, they will obviously be suspicious this time. Once trust has been lost, it is hard to regain. Avoid personal attacks and a 'blame culture'.
Try to ensure your proposals are within peoples' comfort zones (i.e. what they are happy with psychologically).

Consider whether the change should be introduced slowly or in one go. The former allows time for people to be involved and consulted, and to digest, absorb and adjust to the new situation. It can be carried out in stages such as initial awareness, first formal approach, feasibility study, agreed commitment, outline plan, details etc., and facilitates such approaches as dry runs and pilot schemes.

The latter is sometimes called the 'Big Bang' approach, and has the advantages that follow from it being over in one go. Quick adoption and achievements of the benefits of the change, less potential for confusion during an extended transition period, concentrated effort (i.e. no need to maintain the old system while bringing in the new). There is also less chance for resistance to build.

Once the Change has been Agreed and Accepted, it can be Implemented

To avoid possible confusion over responsibility, an individual should always be placed in overall control. Consultants can be used for specialist expertise or experience, or to do the dirty work, but beware of long term consequences previously discussed (i.e. failure to develop internal managers, and undermining the positive attitude to change).

Those affected should be given thorough training in the new systems. This is important to ensure understanding and competence, but also for its psychological effects: it makes them feel important and cared for. It also helps to ensure people do not slip back into the old ways of doing things, which is another aspect of force field analysis: to keep the momentum going, the positive forces must be constantly kept greater than those resisting the change.

Results should be monitored carefully, looking for individuals who are unable to cope with the change, and possible development of negative attitudes, both active and passive.

Boost morale by frequent communication, verbal and written, particularly of success, and reward successful implementation of stages of the plan and eventual completion.

Political withholding of information or selective presentation may be tempting, but is dangerous. People will not be pleased if / when they find out, and long term trust may be threatened.

Implementation is a particularly difficult stage in tackling the problem of global warming, for several reasons:

- many of the potential solutions cost **MONEY**.

- they would have to be introduced globally. It is all very well, for example, for the UK to agree to lessen use of CFCs at the same rate as other countries, the standard of living here is already high. Can we expect countries like China and India to do the same when it would mean their populations continuing to forego such "luxuries" as fridges and cars, in countries which are big, hot and dry? In fact, the USA has refused to carry out the Kyoto agreements on pollution control unless China agrees to cut its use by more than they do.

- the average human seems to be incredibly selfish. Mining companies and unions in America have spent millions on sponsoring research to 'disprove' global warming theories, promoting their views and canvassing in the senate. The NIMBY (Not In My Back Yard) philosophy predominates. If they truly believe in their cause, they cannot really be blamed for hanging on to their gravy train for as long as possible. I am convinced, however, that as was the case with tobacco companies, they know the truth and are willing to jeopardise the future welfare of all flora and fauna on the planet in order to maintain their high incomes.

   But they are not the only ones. Most people seem to have accepted that global warming is occurring, but as previously mentioned, very few have made any major sacrifice such as giving up their car, or even lesser measures such as walking, using public transport or car sharing to get to work.

- Government interference and control is very much out of favour. The collapse of communism, extensive privatisation and competition throughout industry, and the Government's stated policy of reducing governmental interference in people's lives, all lead to this conclusion.

- as discussed under Appreciate and Specify, it is extremely hard to prove a problem exists at all, let alone that it is of catastrophic proportions and requires extremely drastic actions to solve. My own view is that within 50 years this will be a dead planet, but I always was an optimist!

Review
Having implemented the solution, two important stages in the decision making model remain: Review and Learn. While there is no clear cut-off between these, I use Review to only cover assessment of the effectiveness of a particular decision. Learn then looks at whether our future decision making could be improved, and how this should be done.

To assess the effectiveness of a particular decision, it is necessary to establish the extent to which it is being successful: are the desired outcomes and objectives being achieved? For simple decisions, results will often quickly follow implementation, with success or otherwise immediately apparent, and a clear 'cause and effect' relationship established. You decide not to take your umbrella on a walk (because it doesn't need the exercise) and end up rather wet!

More complicated situations may not have such clear-cut, immediate outcomes, and there may be other factors influencing the results. Establishment of the extent to which the result is due to the decision implemented will often require careful analysis, and may not be possible. You might decide to wear a bright tie to an interview: if you get the job, is it because, or in spite of the tie?

Where a solution consists of a number of related activities, the degree of success of each activity should be established. Is the process breaking down at a particular point, and if so: who, what where, why, when, how? Thus, if an organisation's new product fails to achieve anticipated sales levels, analysis should take place as to how successfully it was produced, distributed, advertised and sold. Was the price competitive? Were there quality issues? Was it available in the places where, and at the times when, customers expected? The similarities between this analysis and that carried out at the Causes stage should be apparent.

Solutions may not take effect immediately, and they may have long-term consequences, so their ultimate effectiveness may not be known for some time. It may, however, be possible to assess whether the intended actions have been successfully carried out, and whether particular aspects of the solution are working. For example, the ultimate degree of success of an operation to give someone an artificial knee will not be known for many years, but it should be possible to discover how successful particular aspects were very quickly. How long was the person 'on the list'? Did the operation take place on the date originally scheduled? How long did it take? Were there any immediate complications? How much pain was the patient in, and for how long? (it may be difficult to assess this objectively) How quickly did their mobility improve?

Once the Review stage has been completed, it may be necessary to start the whole decision making process again for the particular problem. This will clearly be the case for those problems where the intended solution has not been successfully implemented, but will also apply for those where solutions are only temporary. For example, organisations constantly go through budgeting cycles, with the outcomes of one year's budgeting and actual activity forming part of the input to the following year's budget preparation. This can be viewed as a constantly repeating problem, or a new problem each year.

Regardless of the above, the Learn stage must not be forgotten.

Problem Solving

Review is very difficult with regard to the solution of global warming due to the measurement and time scale problems previously discussed. Nevertheless, I believe it is reasonable to conclude that we certainly have not taken sufficient actions so far to solve the problem ourselves.

Action has been very limited, but more to the point, seems to have had extremely little, if any, effect on the problem, which is, as far as can be seen, worsening rapidly. Measurements still show increasing average temperatures, melting polar and other ice-caps, rising sea level, and increasing levels of pollutants, particularly the 'green house' gasses. New fears are emerging, such as that the major effect of global warming may be changing rainfall and increased ferocity of storms.

It is extremely unlikely that a man-made permanent solution to a problem of this nature could be found - getting the temperature of the Earth permanently 'right' would be very difficult (as did Goldilocks in the famous story, we want our porridge "not too hot, not too cold, but just right"). It is only likely to be achieved, if at all, by constant intervention, similar to that required for the simple heating system considered at the start of the chapter.

A non-interventionist view here would be that the likelihood of us getting the balance right is far less than that of us making things even worse. Others would argue that God / nature has designed the Earth with in-built mechanisms for keeping it as a suitable environment for life to flourish, and if warming continues, one of these mechanisms will come into action and restore balance.

These issues were discussed in the Specify section, along with the counter-argument that we have already 'intervened' e.g. through using vast amounts of pollutants, and that any natural mechanisms which do exist could have been upset.

The recent television series Earth Story included consideration of why it is that the Earth is 'just right' when Venus is 'too hot' and Mars is 'too cold'. It concluded that it was because of a number of natural phenomena including volcanic activity, tectonic plate movement, abundant water, flora and fauna. Each of these had played a vital part at a particular stage, and all were felt to be important for maintaining the current balance.

One particular balancing mechanism mentioned was that, as temperatures rise, life proliferates and ties up carbon dioxide in the form of fossils. Since carbon dioxide is the main 'greenhouse gas', lessening its concentration in the atmosphere leads to a temperature drop. This links very clearly with the earlier discussion of causes of global warming. A possible problem is that the amount of life on the planet may be approaching maximum, but we are still pumping more carbon dioxide into the atmosphere.

Since the solutions implemented to date are not working, we must go through the process again, looking for improvements and new approaches. I make some suggestions in the Learn section below, but I fear they will prove fruitless. I just do not believe sufficient global actions will be taken unless and until there are several catastrophic events which are unequivocally the result of global warming. By then, it may be too late to take effective action, and in any case the immediate reaction to such disasters would be to cope with their aftermath.

If a major power was very badly affected by such a disaster, it would probably react in a unilateral manner, possibly by invading another, weaker power to grab resources such as fresh water or habitable land. (Australia would seem a likely target if, say Japan was to suddenly lose a high proportion of its land mass). Such action would be likely to lead to major conflict, but certainly not to an immediate world-wide focus on, and reaction to, the underlying cause.

The above discussion was very much at the global level, with the overall conclusion that there is little likelihood of effective action on problems of this nature. This leads to the thought that actions must be taken at the individual level.

It is possible for individuals to take a stand against pollution, and I am all for it, but it is not the point I want to make here. Instead, I want to briefly consider the actions they could take to cope with, or even benefit from global warming given that they accept that it is a genuine problem and insufficient action will be taken to prevent it.

If you accept that temperatures and sea level are rising, move to (or at least buy some land in, and obtain any necessary visas for) an area which is currently cool and well above sea level (Canada?) Protect yourself from increased radiation by wearing stronger sun screen lotion, a large hat and long sleeves.

If you live in an area which could flood, either move, or make sure all flood defences are under good repair, and able to cope with new scenarios, and maintain stocks of food and other necessities. If determined to live there, sell your house and rent instead, thereby passing on the risk.

Look for ways in which to exploit the new situation: start to grow more exotic fruit, open a vineyard, sell sunglasses and ice cream.

If you are extremely pessimistic about the long-term future, make sure you get the most out of the short term: "Don't worry, be happy!"

I will leave you planning your escape, while moving on to the final stage in the ASK SIR L model.

Learn

Having faced and tackled a problem, can we learn from it?

All too often problems are solved after a great deal of thought, time and effort, but little attempt is made to make use of the experience, skills and knowledge gained in the process. This is particularly true of organisations, where the benefits gained by one part are often not promulgated throughout. In order to be a 'learning organisation' steps must be taken to identify and share the learning potential of all activities, including problem solving.

For an individual problem, success or failure is what matters, but if we want to avoid problems of this nature in the future, and improve the quality of our problem solving, we need to identify any shortcomings in our current processes.

There is a clear danger here of being wise after the event, and assuming a successful solution was the right one, or one which failed was wrong. We need to establish the extent to which success or failure was due to the problem solving approach adopted, as opposed to subsequent unforeseen events or plain bad luck. We must consider whether we could improve the likelihood of making successful decisions in the future, given the facts as they were at the time of taking the decision.

Was our approach to the problem valid? We have just worked through the ASK SIR L model, and I think it is rather good! It is my baby, so I would say that - you need to decide whether it is right for you, and the particular problem you are faced with. As will be seen in chapter 5, there are many weaknesses with the logical approach, and circumstances in which alternative approaches such as mind games are superior.

Was the approach carried out correctly? Was the problem's existence recognised as early as possible? Was it specified correctly and accurately? Were all possible causes and solutions correctly identified? Would an alternative decision making technique have proved superior? What information was missing which would have been valuable, and could it be made available in future?

Throughout this analysis, the main focus should be on learning how we can improve our future decision making. Having extracted all available learning points, we must ensure they will be carried forward into our future decision making. In the case of an organisation, this includes spreading the word throughout, and can be achieved in a number of ways including formal, written processes and procedures, education and training, charts, diagrams, models and bullet point lists.

The importance of ensuring communication of the lessons to all those likely to benefit from them cannot be over stated. Systems should be established to confirm that all the above has actually happened, the lessons have been learnt, and problem solving approaches improved. The ultimate test is the quality of future decisions, which should be checked using scenarios and case studies. Waiting to see whether real problems are tackled well may be too late.

Are there lessons to be learnt from the global warming experience? I believe there are plenty!

Complicated problems like this are likely to have a range of viewpoints with regard to their existence, severity, causes and solution. These are further clouded by the vested interest and hidden agendas of various parties. Approaches must be found to enable clarity of thought and analysis to prevail. Permanent monitoring of the health of the planet must be given higher priority.
Our whole approach to the problem has been extremely short-sighted and self centred. Many governments and people have accepted that there is a problem, and that drastic actions need to be taken, but few are willing to actually take them. Much of this revolves around a NIMBY (Not In My Back Yard) attitude and the vested interest referred to above. We must find ways of achieving positive action. People and governments must become more accountable, and accept their role and responsibility for solving global problems. We must find ways to control the extreme selfishness inherent in humanity.

Possibly due to the way in which awareness of the problem has slowly grown, we seem to have accepted it as part of life, and are consequently in danger of ignoring it. It is yesterday's news (have you been guilty of this while reading through the discussion about it? 'Why go on about this? Everyone knows about global warming. It has been talked about for years, and nothing much has changed, so why panic now?') This is a natural human tendency, which we must find ways to overcome if people are to treat this kind of problem seriously.

More generally, global warming has revealed the fragility of the environment, and our historic complacency in assuming that it will look after itself. We must become more aware of, and concerned about, our potential to ruin it. Humanity is now so numerous, and our activity on such a vast scale, that we have the capacity to destroy our God / nature given home.

We must appreciate the fact that we may already be causing other effects. My analysis has focused on the warming effects of pollution, but we also know that destroying the ozone layer is allowing harmful rays to reach the Earth's surface, causing various forms of cancer, blindness and other problems to both humanity and animals. Effects on plants may be equally severe, but less easily identified.

Pollution also directly causes such illnesses as cancer. On many occasions, I have sat in traffic queues watching the fumes pouring out of the exhaust of the vehicle in front, wondering what harm is being done to my lungs.

Genetically modified (GM) crops are being introduced throughout the world with no real proof that they will not have harmful side effects. Scientists have just finished mapping human DNA, giving us the potential to experiment with the structure of future generations. "How many arms do you want for this one, Mrs Robinson?"

Ways must be found to control all such developments in a far more rigorous manner.

Next Steps

This chapter has given detailed consideration to the 7 stages of decision making. Chapters 3 and 4 focus on particular elements, decision making and risk management respectively. Decision making considers ways in which choice can be made between various possible solutions, while risk management deals with identification and consideration of the likelihood of particular problems arising, and ways of lessening their consequences.

Review Questions

2.1 What 7 stages are suggested for logical problem solving? If you don't know, ASK SIR L (and no chocolate for a week).

2.2 What do you think is the most difficult part of Appreciate / Specify? Did I define the global warming problem sufficiently at that stage?

2.3 What additional potential causes of global warming did you identify? (If the answer is none, go to jail without passing go!)

2.4 Were any of the weightings I used particularly inaccurate in your opinion?

2.5 Are you as optimistic as I am about finding and implementing a solution to the global warming problem?

Exercises

2.1 Place your own weightings on the actual causes of global warming. How would your weightings affect the viability of my suggested solutions? What solutions would you suggest to deal with the causes you identify?
(There is no answer provided for this exercise).

2.2 The M25 ('Magic Roundabout' ring road round London) is gaining reputation as the biggest car park in the world and it has been suggested that people will be born / get married / have kids / divorce / die whilst sitting in the same traffic jam if things get much worse. Carry out a logical problem analysis to tackle the problem of congestion on the M25.

This is your chance to try out the ASK SIR L model in practice. I provide a fairly detailed 'answer' but to do it justice, you might want to spend an hour on each stage, recording your thoughts as you go. Don't read my answer until you have finished your own (you can continue reading the rest of the book while gathering your thoughts.)

Answers to Exercises

2.2 CONGESTION ON THE M25

Clearly, there is no perfect answer to this problem, but the following notes are my thoughts:

Appreciate
I know I told you there was a problem, so have carried out this stage for you to some extent, but I assume you were already aware that considerable delay and frustration existed.

Specify
Attempting to deal with general traffic congestion would be very different to looking exclusively at that on the M25, so an important first step will be deciding where to place the boundary on the problem. I have kept to the M25, so congestion on other roads has not been considered except to the extent it could affect M25 levels.

Clarifying the precise problem to be tackled might focus on:
- Drivers need / wish to get to work etc.
- Traffic cannot move as fast as drivers wish to
- Research required to establish facts as opposed to hearsay. I have not done this, so all comments made are purely my own guesses, but it may be that the following was revealed:
- Particularly bad during morning and evening rush hours (say 6.30 - 9.30 am and 4.30 - 7.00 p.m.);
- Fairly clear between, say 9 p.m. and 6 am;
- Certain bottleneck areas: junctions; stretch between M1 and M4 junctions; long hills; roadworks;
- Worse in winter and during bad weather;
- Crashes often partly to blame (congestion often worse on other carriageway due to 'rubber-necking'!)

What would be regarded as a successful solution to the problem? This is a difficult area in its own right, since there are so many types of user all with their own driving habits, speeds and objectives. For the typical car driver, it might be 'An average speed of 60 mph, for 95% of rush hour journeys', although you will see clear weaknesses and problems in measuring successful achievement. For example, it is often said that objectives should be SMART - Specific, Measurable, Achievable, Relevant and Time-related: the suggested objective does not achieve all of these attributes.

Is perception worse than reality? People may overstate the true extent of delays, forgetting all the good journeys and constantly reliving the occasional 'nightmare trip'.

A completely different approach would be to challenge the whole idea that there is a problem to be solved! It is often argued that traffic volume increases until road capacity is reached / exceeded. Thus improving conditions on the M25 would just encourage more use, and congestion would soon return. Linking this to the global warming issue, the argument would be that the last thing we should do is improve the roads. This is, however, wandering towards the more general 'dealing with all traffic congestion' problem that I said I would not be covering.

Causes
The following table summarises my thoughts, and is explained below.

Potential Major Causes	Possible	Actual	Weighting
Too many users	Y	Y	.35
Wrong type of user	Y	Y	.20
Bad weather / lighting	Y	N	.05
Bad design	Y	Y	.15
High accident levels	Y	N	.10
Misuse	Y	Y	.15

The M25 was originally intended to keep traffic out of central London e.g. by allowing traffic from the Channel ports heading north to bypass. In practice, however:

- the volume of traffic was vastly underestimated by the planners. This seems to be a tradition for road planners, and could be contrasted with the fantastic forward thinking by Victorian engineers, who designed such major works as the London sewers, on a sufficient scale to cope with the high growth in usage;
- many users make local journeys, only staying on for one or two junctions. This causes particular problems as vehicles entering or exiting tend to slow the overall traffic flow, once a standstill occurs there is a rapid build up of delay as people negotiate with each other, and junctions are notorious accident 'black spots';
- much of the problem is in the 'rush hour', with many commuters travelling one per car. Parents on 'the school run' cause problems on both of the latter counts.

Many users drive in a manner which exacerbates the problem. I am sure you have a few favourites of your own, but some of mine are (I don't mean these are things I do, of course. Like yours, my driving is exemplary. It is all those others...):

- staying in middle / outside lanes when the inside lane is free and faster vehicles are trying to pass. This seems to be a particular trait of driving in Britain, German drivers for example, being keen to get out of the fast-lane once they have carried out an overtaking manoeuvre. It results not only in effectively reducing the width of the road from 3 to 2 lanes, but also encourages frustrated drivers to pass on the wrong side - known as 'undertaking' to distinguish it from the correct 'overtaking' but also to highlight how dangerous it is - likely to result in a visit to the undertakers;

- sudden lane changes e.g. cutting in from the outside lane in the last 50 yards before the desired exit, having just made it past a vehicle in the middle lane. Often accompanied by hitting the brakes in preparation for taking the exit curve;
- not letting people into their lane. This may be a reason why people are loathe to use the inside lane: concerned that they may not be allowed out if they want to overtake;
- drivers of slow vehicles overtaking each other while going up a long hill, the overtaking vehicle being only slightly faster and consequently taking forever to get past, and holding up the faster traffic;
- Many cars speed along at close to 100 mph until they hit the next hold up, where they are reduced to an average, say 10 mph. If they travelled at a constant 60mph most of the jams might disappear, along with the driver's frustration. Likelihood and consequences of accidents would also lessen, and the overall effect on traffic flow could be dramatic. Most individuals would probably accept this logic, but the problem is getting everyone to behave rationally. If an individual drove at the suggested 60, they would be overtaken by all those going faster, and still be held up by the jam they create.

Bad weather causes frequent minor delays (rain) and occasional major ones (fog; ice; snow).

Design faults include some 2-lane stretches and poor junctions, probably resulting from poor prediction of utilisation levels in general, and in specific sections.

Solutions

As shown above, I feel the main causes to be too many users (i.e. vehicles) at peak times, and many of those users being 'the wrong type'. These could be tackled by measures such as:

- only vehicles with 3+ people in may use the fast lane in peak hours;
- general encouragement of multiple occupancy of vehicles: advertising; official pick up points; agreed fares to vehicle owners;
- better public transport: speed; frequency; comfort; access; low / zero fares;
- staggered working hours, and increased home working (which may occur naturally due to the effects of IT such as e-commerce).

While I do not view it as a major contributory factor, the effect of bad weather could be lessened by improved lighting (both of the road and on vehicles), better drainage; faster reaction e.g. salt / grit / snow ploughs; and better warnings e.g. of fog ahead, which is done particularly badly at present, with electronic warning signs spaced so far apart, and so frequently not reflecting reality, that people tend to ignore them.

Implementation

Attempts are constantly being made to deal with particular bottleneck areas, by introducing additional lanes, varying speed limits, highlighting alternative routes, improving signage, and generally attempting to keep traffic flowing. A particularly important illustration is the Dartford crossing of the river Thames. I have always found it amazing that the main road link between Europe and the North of England / Scotland has a toll tunnel in the middle of it! At one stage, this caused regular delays of upwards of an hour, but these have virtually disappeared since the opening of the Queen Elizabeth II Bridge.

Some of the potential solutions would require very careful handling. Would it be possible to enforce rules such as 'only vehicles with 3+ people in may use the fast lane in peak hours' mentioned previously? (I believe it is used in several major cities in the US, including Los Angeles). Would the pick-up points be misused? Would the fare be fair to taxi drivers? Are there potential insurance problems?

Successive governments have been inexplicably biased against public transport, keeping subsidies minimal while spending vast amounts on roads, despite the environmental arguments in favour.

Review
Unless very dramatic / fundamental changes in attitudes to the use of vehicles take place, congestion on the M25 is likely to be a permanent problem, with short term solutions aimed at dealing with specific issues as they come to the fore.

In fact, I believe the extent of queuing and other delays has reduced in recent years, so would say measures taken have been successful to at least some degree. The main problem currently seems to be the north-west corner, around the M4 / M40, but improvements are being implemented there too.

Learn
Politics is a balancing game, and long term solutions to problems of this nature would probably require more radical, drastic action than any government would be willing to take. One only has to look at the attitude of drivers to increases in petrol prices to see that any government taking such action would be risking 'political suicide'.

To change such attitudes, the case for action would have to be made much more convincingly than it has to date, and continually reinforced. This is unlikely to come from one of the main political parties, and 'The Greens' have been doing their best for many years. It may be that people are complacent, and it will take a catastrophic natural disaster to convince them to really care, and take, or at least accept action.

It may be possible to improve future planning, so as to better predict actual usage levels and likely bottlenecks. 20:20 hindsight is commonly available, and it is in reality extremely difficult to anticipate such variables. A particular factor here is the time scale involved: the M25 was completed in the early 1980s, but sections were open years earlier, and the main planning phase was in the mid 1970s.

Given the difficulty of accurate long term forecasting, three basic approaches are apparent: build to cope with volumes far above anticipated levels, search for flexible solutions, and / or respond to events as they occur. The former may help with the particular problem, but could be very wasteful of scarce resources if such heavy demand did not materialise. Flexible solutions are ideal, and would include such steps as to design the road in such a way that it could be easily widened, and to purchase the necessary land, using it for other relatively short-term purposes pending its requirement for additional lanes. Responding to actual demand and circumstances is the main, obvious approach adopted.

Finally, perhaps we need to be more realistic in our expectations. I recall travelling from Essex, on the east side of London, to Heathrow airport, on the west, around 1980, prior to the M25 being opened. It took 3 hours and was terrible. The same trip now takes an average of 1 hour, and the most common delays take place on the final spur road leading to the airport. The M25 has been a fantastic success!

Chapter 3
Decision Making

I used to think I was indecisive, but now I'm not so sure.

I do hope that is not how you feel after reading chapter 2, but if it is, this chapter should put you right.

As stated in the previous chapter, I am using the term decision making to refer to the process of choosing between options. In many instances, this will be done as part of the Solutions stage of problem solving, but often there will not be a problem to be solved as such, just the fact that we are faced with a choice of possible actions and need to decide between them. It could be argued that 'the problem' is 'deciding between solutions', which would highlight the fact that even simple decisions should be preceded by specification of objectives and generation of solutions.

Decision making covers such possibilities as where to go skiing, whether to change jobs, or whether more money should be spent on education, and I shall take the first of these as an illustration.

Where to go Skiing

Specify Objectives / Requirements

Deciding where to go skiing implies an earlier decision has been taken: to go skiing. For me, that is not so much a decision as a fact of life, but for others it might entail a fine balance between all sorts of holidays. If thinking of going for the first time, factors such as fear of injury and judging likely ability and enjoyment levels would come into play.

An important aspect of decision making is keeping yourself focused on the decision in hand. It would be easy to keep drifting: before deciding where to ski, we must decide whether to ski, and before that, whether to take a holiday, and before that, how secure our job is, and before that.... I must keep focused: I am looking at where to go skiing.

Initially, objectives and basic requirements should be established. Objectives will depend on the individuals involved, their experience, ages, attitudes and resources. Are they 'snow plough fodder' (beginners), 'powder pigs' (experts looking for off-piste action), or 'board stupid' (snow boarders)? Is it crucial that top quality skiing is available, or do they want a balance between good skiing, other activities, and night life?

Having thought about and clarified objectives, the requirements most likely to result in their achievement can be established. This could include:

- quality / variety / number of runs and lifts;
- location (country, region, height);
- dates / duration;
- accommodation (hotel / chalet; room size / occupancy; with private bath / shower; full / half board / bed and breakfast);
- distance from runs;
- quality of equipment and lessons (if needed);
- night life / restaurants;
- cost;
- travel time / methods.

Can you think of, say 4 I have missed?

Develop Solutions

Many possibilities exist for solving the problem in hand, ranging from a weekend in Scotland, through a week in the Alps, to a fortnight in Canada, the USA or New Zealand, or even...

Sources of information abound, including ski brochures, advice from travel agents and / or friends, own knowledge and experience, research on the internet, watching travel programmes and attending ski shows.

Whilst carrying out this research, it is important to bear in mind what information is required. Much of this may be obtained from a single source (say, ski brochure) but most often it will be necessary to supplement this with personal notes. Design of a standard format can simplify this task, and help ensure all aspects are covered. The amount of time and effort put into fact gathering will depend on a range of factors including extent of experience, importance of getting it right, personal psychology, and your role in the decision. Many individuals effectively leave the decision to their partner - then moan if anything goes wrong.

Select Best

In all but the most obvious decisions, it will be impossible fully to meet all these requirements, so a decision model is required. One approach is to prioritise factors and identify the solution which best meets the highest priorities.

A variation on this is to adopt a two-stage process. Each factor is given a weight to reflect its importance, then each solution is given a raw score under each factor to reflect how well it achieves that requirement. Multiplying the raw scores by the weights, then adding the results, gives a weighted score for how well each solution achieves the overall objectives. For the skiing holiday this could result in:

Table of Raw Scores (out of 10)

Factor	Holiday 1	Holiday 2	Holiday 3	Holiday 4
Location	7	6	8	8
Accommodation	9	8	7	9
Night Life	7	6	8	6
Cost	6	7	5	7

Table of Weighted Scores

Factor	Weight	Holiday 1	Holiday 2	Holiday 3	Holiday 4
Location	0.4	2.8	2.4	3.2	3.2
Accommodation	0.3	2.7	2.4	2.1	2.7
Night Life	0.2	1.4	1.2	1.6	1.2
Cost	0.1	0.6	0.7	0.5	0.7
Total	1.0	7.5	6.7	7.4	7.8

To illustrate the calculation, holiday 1 scored 7 for location, which had a weighting of 0.4, so holiday 1's weighted score for that factor was 7x0.4 = 2.8.

As part of this evaluation, attempts should be made to tackle any weaknesses inherent in particular alternatives. If an option appears to have a poor night life, could you do something to improve it?!

This approach attempts to inject some objectivity into decision making, and often helps identify solutions which are clearly not optimal. Its major weakness is that, in reality, it is still based on subjective weightings and raw scores, so the objectivity is largely illusory. Numerical factors such as cost can often be given very precise scores, but difficulty occurs with factors such as quality, taste and fear.

Another weakness is that it can over-complicate decision making: agreeing weightings for each factor and raw scores for each solution can be time consuming, particularly where there are a large number of factors.

Where two or more solutions have similar weighted total scores, there is invariably debate as to the validity of the underlying raw data. This can be useful, however, as it helps bring out true feelings. Sometimes a particular solution scores highest, but those making the decision agree that a different solution is actually preferable, due to some inexpressible 'factor x'.

Additional complexity arises when more than one person's circumstances and requirements have to be met. For example, how could my desire for challenging runs be compared with your desire for quality night life and other peoples' limited funds and fear of flying? In such circumstances, negotiation and compromise will be necessary in order for a decision acceptable to everyone to be agreed. This problem is covered in more detail in chapter 6.

Where there are a multitude of possible solutions, selection can be carried out in phases. One approach here is to initially complete a quick, rough analysis of each option, eliminating any obviously unsuitable ones, with subsequent analysis becoming increasingly detailed so as to eliminate more and more options until only one is left. Another is to break down the solution into several parts, and tackle each in turn. With the ski holiday, it may be possible to initially agree dates, country and type of accommodation, thereby narrowing down the search.

Problems with scoring subjective factors and solutions is one reason why decision making in the public sector is often difficult. Funds are always limited, but how can a fair decision be made between such marginal decisions as having another policeman 'on the beat', two extra school teachers, or another hospital bed?

In practice, such diverse decisions tend to be separated by initially deciding total allocation to each major service area, here law and order, education and health. The same process is then repeated for allocations between elements of that service. Even so, each of these splits is still highly subjective.

One approach is for a number of individuals to complete the scoring exercise, their results being averaged to give an overall score for the subjective elements of the decision. This can then be combined with the scores for any numerical elements, and a decision taken.

Given that this type of decision is political, a political approach can also be used. Individuals vote for the party they believe will make decisions most in line with their wishes. The party gaining most votes is elected, and is expected to carry out the policies stated in their manifesto. If the people do not like what they do, they can vote for a different party next time.

This system is very bad, but it is the best anyone has come up with! There is a clear danger that the majority could elect a party which then acted unfairly towards those groups or attitudes which it did not represent or support.

Having made the decision, the remaining three stages of problem solving (which are?) come into play, and all the points made in chapter 2 are relevant.

Numerical Analysis
When faced with a problem or decision, it is often possible to use a numerical approach to calculate either the correct solution, or at least the likely results of various actions.

The remainder of this chapter examines Probability and Algebra, two numerical approaches frequently used in decision making, before illustrating how useful computer spreadsheets are when dealing with numerical calculations. Chapter 4 looks at risk analysis and includes the numerical approach known as Expected Values.

Probability

Very often, when making a decision, we need to consider how likely particular outcomes are. To do this scientifically, we need to use the statistical technique of Probability.

What is the probability of a slice of toast falling 'jam side down'?

Starting with a very simple illustration, if you spin a coin, what is the probability of it landing on heads?

Assuming it is not 'double-headed', and cannot land on its side, disappear down a drain etc., there are 2 possible outcomes, heads or tails, each of equal likelihood. The stated assumptions may seem obvious, and will certainly be accepted as valid here, but one should always consider the unexpected.

The probability of heads is 1 in 2, or $^1/_2$, and the probability of tails is also $^1/_2$. In order to help ensure all possible outcomes have been included in an analysis, probabilities are usually expressed so that the combined probability of all possible outcomes totals 1. This can be clearly seen here: probability of heads + probability of tails = $^1/_2$ + $^1/_2$ = 1.

Confusion can be caused by different ways of expressing the same probability, with $1/2$ sometimes denoted as 0.5, or 50%. Hopefully you can see that 0.5 + 0.5 = 1.0, and 50% + 50% = 100% = 1, so are able to rise above such feeble attempts.

What is the Probability of Obtaining Heads 4 Times in a Row?

On each occasion, probability of heads is $1/2$. The probability of this happening 4 times in a row is $1/2 \times 1/2 \times 1/2 \times 1/2$, which can be expressed as $(1/2)^4$ and is $1/16$, or 0.0625, or 6.25%. Thus, to determine the probability of several independent event all occurring, we multiply their individual probabilities together. Not surprisingly, this is often known as the multiplication rule. If 1 person in 3 drinks tea, and one in four has a sandwich, the chances of an individual having tea and a sandwich is $1/3 \times 1/4 = 1/12$. We must be very careful, however, that the events really are independent: is choice of drink independent of choice of food?

If You Have Thrown Heads 3 Times in a Row, What is the Chance of Heads Next Time?

Past results (unless they make us conclude the coin is biased!) do not affect future ones, so the answer is $1/2$. Starting from scratch, 4 heads in a row only has $1/16$ probability, but we have started here with 3 in a row already, a $1/8$ chance, which, with the $1/2$ probability of heads next time comes back to $1/16$.

This is the same logic as makes it at all rational for a person to enter the national lottery. The chances of any particular 6 numbers being randomly selected out of 49 is about 1 in 14 million. (Calculation of the exact chances of winning, and discussion as to whether it is completely rational to enter the lottery are covered later in this chapter and in chapter 5 respectively). You select your 6 numbers, then hope the 1 in 14 million chance of those numbers being selected by the machine occurs.

Decision Making

You can select any 6 numbers you want, so there is not 1 in 14 million chance of you getting that right! If the chances of you winning relied on you getting the right 6 numbers on your card (1 in 14 million) then those same numbers coming up (1 in 14 million) i.e. (1 in 14 million) x (1 in 14 million) = 1 in 196 thousand billion (American) entering would be more or less a straight donation!

This may seem a ridiculous illustration since it is so obvious that when you select your numbers it has no effect on their likelihood of coming up. I would be tempted to agree, yet some people will not enter the lottery by way of a 'lucky dip' (where the computer randomly selects 6 numbers for the entrant) since they believe it is highly unlikely for the same 6 numbers to be generated twice in a row. This is illogical, however, since once the numbers have been selected, whether by you, your aunt Sally, the grocer's pet snake, or a machine, they have the same 1 in 14 million chance of immediate re-selection as does any other set of 6 numbers.

Probabilities based on dice are calculated in similar fashion to those for coins, but the probability of a particular number coming up on any throw is only $\frac{1}{6}$. This results in the following illustrative probabilities:

- Throw a 6: $\frac{1}{6}$
- Throw four 6s in a row: $(\frac{1}{6})\times(\frac{1}{6})\times(\frac{1}{6})\times(\frac{1}{6}) = (\frac{1}{6})^4 = \frac{1}{1296}$

What Probability is There of Throwing 7 with 2 Die?

Whatever number the first dice lands on, the other dice could make the total 7, but could only do so with one specific number e.g. if the first was 4, the second would have to be 3. Thus, the probability is $\frac{1}{6}$.

Similar logic can be applied to calculate the chances of obtaining any particular result when throwing two die. Provided the first dice leaves from 1 to 6 remaining to achieve the target number, the second dice has a 1/6 chance of getting it. We need to work out the probability of the first number leaving from 1 to 6 outstanding, then apply the 1/6 probability of the second dice being 'right'. For example, a total of 2 can only be achieved if the first dice gives 1, leaving the second to give 1 also.

Target	First Dice	Resultant Probability
2	1	$1/6 \times 1/6 = 1/36$
3	1 or 2	$2/6 \times 1/6 = 2/36$
4	1,2 or 3	$3/6 \times 1/6 = 3/36$
5	1,2,3 or 4	$4/6 \times 1/6 = 4/36$
6	1,2,3,4 or 5	$5/6 \times 1/6 = 5/36$
7	1,2,3,4,5 or 6	$6/6 \times 1/6 = 6/36$
8	2,3,4,5 or 6	$5/6 \times 1/6 = 5/36$
9	3,4,5 or 6	$4/6 \times 1/6 = 4/36$
10	4,5 or 6	$3/6 \times 1/6 = 3/36$
11	5 or 6	$2/6 \times 1/6 = 2/36$
12	6	$1/6 \times 1/6 = 1/36$

Several points are worth observing:

There is a great deal of symmetry in the results, probabilities increasing at first, then decreasing, by $1/36$ each time. This is typical of probability distributions.

Because for a particular total, we need the first dice to obtain a given result, and the second to then make this up to the required total, the combined probability of the two independent events occurring is given by multiplying their individual probabilities together.

If, instead, we are calculating the probability of one of several possible outcomes occurring, we add together their individual probabilities. This is known as the addition rule, and applies where the individual outcomes are mutually exclusive (i.e. they cannot both occur, which is the case here, since we cannot throw, say 7 and 9 at the same time).

The addition rule can be illustrated and verified by adding together the probabilities of all possible outcomes, here giving a total $^{36}/_{36}$, or 1, which also confirms that we have covered all possible outcomes, and calculated their probabilities correctly. A further illustration would be to determine the probability of obtaining, say a total of either 5, 7 or 8. Adding together their individual probabilities gives $^{4}/_{36}$ + $^{6}/_{36}$ + $^{5}/_{36}$ = $^{15}/_{36}$. We would expect the probability of obtaining any other result (2, 3, 4, 6, 9, 10, 11 or 12) to be $^{21}/_{36}$ to add back to the total $^{36}/_{36}$ for all possible outcomes, and by golly it is!

What is the Probability of 2 Days Chosen At Random Both Being Fridays?
The answer seems to be obvious, 1 chance in seven each time:
$^{1}/_{7}$ x $^{1}/_{7}$ = $^{1}/_{49}$

Of course, we must be careful to ensure the days really are random. The probability of 2 days next week both being Fridays is zero, since there is only one Friday each week! Similarly, from your viewpoint, the chances of my birthday being on Friday next year, and Saturday the following year might at first sight appear to be $^{1}/_{7}$ x $^{1}/_{7}$ = $^{1}/_{49}$, but in fact, in a normal year there are 365 days which is 52 weeks plus 1 day. Thus, in 3 out of 4 years, a Saturday birthday must follow a Friday one in the previous year. When the Leap Year takes effect, a Saturday birthday will definitely not follow a Friday one.

Overall, from your viewpoint, there is a $^{1}/_{7}$ probability of my birthday being on a Friday next year, and if that does occur, $^{3}/_{4}$ probability of the next being on a Saturday, giving a combined probability of $^{1}/_{7}$ x $^{3}/_{4}$ = $^{3}/_{28}$. So if I offered you odds of 100 to 1 that my birthday will not be on Friday next year and Saturday the year after, how much would you be willing to stake?

In the above discussion (I always laugh to myself when I write that. Why are you reading a book written by someone who discusses things with himself? Particularly when, unbeknown to you, I often lose the argument!) I twice said 'from your viewpoint'. This was to further emphasise the importance of ensuring we are genuinely being random when dealing with probabilities. From my viewpoint, I may know what day of the week my birthday is on next year, and you can be sure I definitely would before offering you such generous odds! Now, did you say £100?

(No, this is not a genuine offer to stand for all time. You might be as tricky as I am, and hang on until my birthday does meet the criteria).

What is the Probability of Obtaining At Least One 5 when Rolling 2 Die?

There is a $1/6$ or $6/36$ probability of the first roll being a 5, in which case it does not matter what the second is.

If the first is not a 5, a probability of $5/6$, we require the second to be a 5, probability $1/6$, combined probability $5/6 \times 1/6 = 5/36$.

In total, we achieve at least one five on $6/36 + 5/36 = 11/36$ occasions.

Notice that it would have been wrong to calculate the probability of at least one 5 as $1/6$ (first dice) + $1/6$ (second dice) = $2/6$ or $12/36$. This is because, on $1/36$ occasions, both dice would give 5, so that occasion uses up 2 of the available 12 5s.

Join the Cue

Imagine you have a bag full of snooker balls, 1 white, 1 black, 1 pink, 1 blue, 1 brown, 1 green, 1 yellow and 15 reds. If you take 1 out at a time:

a) How many do you have to take out to be certain of obtaining a red one?
b) What probability would there be of taking the black, then pink, then blue?
c) What is the probability of the first 3 balls all being red?
d) What is the probability of drawing all the red balls before any of the others?

Taking these in turn:

a) How many do you have to take out to be certain of obtaining a red one?

There are 7 balls that are not red, so they could be the first 7 drawn, thus 8 draws are required to be certain of having at least one red ball.

b) What probability would there be of taking the black, then pink, then blue?

For the first draw, there is 1 black out of a total of 22 balls: $1/22$.

If the black appears, there are 21 balls left for the second draw, only 1 being pink: $1/21$.

The pink having been drawn, the probability of now drawing the blue is $1/20$.

Probability of all 3 occurring in that order:
$1/22 \times 1/21 \times 1/20 = 1/9240$ = not very likely!

Note that if it didn't matter which order the balls were drawn, the probability would be:

First draw: any of the 3 out of 22: $3/22$
Second draw: either of the other 2 out of 21: $2/21$
Third draw: the remaining 1 out of 20: $1/20$

Probability of obtaining the 3 balls in any order:
$3/22 \times 2/21 \times 1/20 = 1/9240$

This is 6 times as likely as the specific order situation, which agrees with the fact that we had 3 times the probability of getting the first draw right, and 2 times for the second draw: 3 x 2 = 6.

These ideas can be used to illustrate two of the basic rules of probability. To do so, I must introduce the idea of 'factorials'. In mathematics, y! stands for y factorial, and means 'multiply the number which y represents by y-1, then y-2, y-3... all the way down to 1'. Thus, 6! is 6x5x4x3x2x1.

The probability of selecting r particular items, in a specific order, out of a total of n items is $^{(n-r)!}/_{n!}$ This may look scary if you are not hot on maths, but taking the 'black then pink then blue' illustration we would have $^{19!}/_{22!}$ Top and bottom both include 19x18x17x16......x2x1, and those parts cancel each other out. That just leaves $^{1}/_{(22x21x20)}$ which is $^{1}/_{9240}$ as shown above.

If we want r specific items out of a total of n items, but they can be in any order, the formula becomes $^{[r!(n-r)!]}/_{n!}$ So, probability of black, pink and blue in any order is $^{(3!19!)}/_{22!}$ Cancelling out the top and bottom 19! leaves $^{(3x2x1)}/_{(22x21x20)}$ which is $^{6}/_{9240}$ as previously calculated.

c) What is the probability of the first 3 balls all being red?

For the first draw, there are 15 reds out of 22 balls, i.e. probability $^{15}/_{22}$
If that is red, there remain 14 reds out of 21 balls i.e. probability $^{14}/_{21}$.
If that is also red, 13 reds remain out of 20 balls: i.e. probability $^{13}/_{20}$.

The probability of all 3 being red is:
$^{15}/_{22}$ x $^{14}/_{21}$ x $^{13}/_{20}$ = $^{2730}/_{9240}$ = 0.2954545

If you want the formula (mathematical maniac that you are) it is
$^{[m!/(m-r)!]}/_{[n!/(n-r)!]}$

with   m   the number of items of the type required (red balls),
            n   the total number of all items (balls),
and   r   the number of items (balls) being selected.

So we would have $^{[15!/12!]}/_{[22!/19!]}$, which looks much worse than it is. As soon as we cancel out the top and bottom repeated bits, all that is left is $^{(15 \times 14 \times 13)}/_{(22 \times 21 \times 20)}$. That is the same as above, and gives $^{2730}/_{9240}$.

d) What is the probability of drawing all the red balls before any of the others?

For the first draw   15 red out of 22 balls
For the second draw   14 red out of 21 balls
For the third draw   13 red out of 20 balls
And so on.

The answer is (keeping numbers for each draw above each other to highlight how they were obtained):

<u>15x</u> <u>14x</u> <u>13x</u> <u>12x</u> <u>11x</u> <u>10x</u> <u>9x</u> <u>8x</u> <u>7x</u> <u>6x</u> <u>5x</u> <u>4x</u> <u>3x</u> <u>2x</u> <u>1</u>
22x 21x 20x 19x 18x 17x 16x 15x 14x 13x 12x 11x 10x 9x 8

Note that "15x14x13x12x11x10x9x8" appears on both the top and bottom, so can be cancelled out. The fraction then becomes:

<u>7x6x5x4x3x2x1</u>   =   <u>5040</u>   = $^{1}/_{170544}$
22x21x20x19x18x17x16   859541760

In fact thinking about the problem the other way round, we could have asked 'what probability that the last 7 balls would be the 7 non-red ones?' which would lead directly to the above fraction.

Using the formula approach: $^{[m!/(m-r)!]}/_{[n!/(n-r)!]}$

with m=7, r=7 and n=22, this gives $^{[7!/0!]}/_{[22!/15!]}$
0! is 1, so we are left with $^{7!}/_{[22!/15!]}$. Cancelling out 15! from the lower section leaves the fraction determined logically before:

       <u>7x 6x 5x 4x 3x 2x1</u>   =   1/170544
       22x21x20x19x18x17x16

"I put 6 pairs in. What is the probability of getting 12 odd ones out?"

Probability of Winning the Lottery

As promised earlier in the chapter, I will now calculate the probability of selecting the same 6 numbers out of 47 as those chosen by the lottery machine. Now that you are a PAP (Probability Aware Person) you could, of course, do it yourself very easily, so why not have a go before reading on?

Decision Making

For the first draw, there are 49 available numbers, and any of your 6 numbers could be chosen: $^6/_{49}$. If you are lucky with that one, for the second draw, chance becomes $^5/_{48}$. Continuing with this logic, the probability of getting all 6 right is

$$\frac{6 \times 5 \times 4 \times 3 \times 2 \times 1}{49 \times 48 \times 47 \times 46 \times 45 \times 44} = \frac{720}{10068347520} = \frac{1}{13983815}$$

Using the formula approach, $^{[r!(n-r)!]}/_{n!}$ would give $^{(6! \times 43!)}/_{49!}$. Cancelling out the top and bottom 43! leaves the above fraction.

So, your chances of winning first prize in the lottery are just a bit better than 1 in 14 million. Before entering, you might also want to consider the fact that even if you do win, it is likely that one or more other people will win too, so you will have to share the prize money. In practice, many people select birthdays, children's ages and such like for their numbers, so it is possible to reduce the likelihood of someone else winning with you by deliberately selecting high numbers which cannot be birthdays etc.. Many people know this tactic, however, and only pick high numbers, so you might want a mix of some high and some low. Again, this is a known tactic, so you might . . .

Algebra

Many problems can be solved using algebra, which is where one derives formulae for the relationships between variables, then uses them to work out the value of each variable in particular circumstances. The problem must be very well defined (Specification stage) and valid Solutions are usually relatively easy to verify. You may recall spending hours of fun at school working out sums like this:

- 4 Apples and 3 Bananas cost 125p
- 2 Apples and 5 Bananas cost 115p
- How much would each cost individually?

This is a simple (oh yes it is!) algebra problem:
$4A + 3B = 125$ formula 1
$2A + 5B = 115$ formula 2

Solution relies on the fact that, for our particular situation, the values of A and B must be the same in both formulas. This is termed 'simultaneous equations', and leads to two common approaches to solution.

In the first approach, we rearrange one formula so that one of the variables is expressed in terms of the other. This can then be substituted into the other formula, leaving only one variable therein. Its value can then be determined, and used to work out the value of the other.

Rearranging formula 2, we have
$5B = 115 - 2A$

Divide by 5:
$B = 23 - 0.4A$

Putting this value for B in formula 1, we have
$4A + 3(23 - 0.4A) = 125$
$4A + 69 - 1.2A = 125$
$4A - 1.2A = 125 - 69$
$2.8A = 56$
$A = 20$

So, an apple costs 20p.

Putting this value for A in formula 1 (I could have chosen formula 2):
4A + 3B = 125
80 + 3B = 125
3B = 125 - 80
3B =   45
B =   15

So, a banana costs 15p

Which we can check using formula 2:
2A + 5B = 115
40 + 75 = 115

Correct. Have a banana!

The second approach involves playing with the formulas by multiplying and dividing until both have the same number of As or Bs. Once this is done, we can subtract one from the other, thereby eliminating either A or B. This is easier than it sounds:

4A + 3B = 125   formula 1
2A + 5B = 115   formula 2

doubling each term in formula 2 gives:
4A + 10B = 230   formula 2a

Subtracting formula 1 from formula 2a leaves:
7B = 105

Thus B = 15 as previously. We can then substitute this value into one of the original formulae, and cross check as before.

The solution to some problems can be too obvious:

If it Takes 2 Women 6 Hours to Dig a Hole, How Long Would it Take 4 Women?

In this case one is tempted to say 3 hours without really thinking about it (i.e. 2 women take 6 hours, a total of 12 woman hours, so 4 would require 12/4 = 3 hours each).

But is it valid to assume every woman can dig as well as every other? And what if the hole is only wide enough for 2 to be in at a time? Or now that there are four people available they decide to play cards instead!

Computers

Debate is taking place as to how 'clever' computers can become, some people (me being one of them) thinking that there is no reason why they should not ultimately be able to make the same kind of 'fuzzy' decisions as humans do. (A fuzzy decision is one where there is no obvious set of decision rules which can be applied logically and rigidly, often because much of the information available is uncertain or guesswork).

If a football is punted up field by the goalkeeper, the opposing centre back uses past experience of the flight of a ball through the air, applied to current conditions such as wind speed and how hard the ball seemed to be kicked, to decide roughly where it will land. She will decide whether to attempt to head it clear, or leave it to another defender. Assuming she decides to go for the ball, as it approaches, she will constantly check its flight and adjust her calculations and position. (How did you react to the idea that the football defender was a woman? Did it challenge your assumption that it would be a man?)

Clearly, the defender does not use actual mathematical equations to do all this, but a series of approximate judgements which become increasingly precise as the degree of uncertainty decreases. Some people believe that this kind of decision making cannot be done by computers. I believe that is nonsense!

There is no reason to assume computers cannot be programmed to learn from experience, develop suitable decision rules, and apply them repeatedly as a situation develops so as to gradually refine an initially rough solution. This approach is, in fact, being used by programmers, and is known as 'fuzzy logic'.

One variation is to apply the concepts of evolution and survival of the fittest to computer programmes. An initial model can be set up to solve a particular problem, say landing a plane. The model is deliberately left flexible, so that many different approaches and results will occur if the model is run thousands or millions of times, against known variations of conditions in which a plane may attempt to land (wind speed and direction, air temperature, rain or snow...). Only those versions of the model which land the plane safely with a high enough frequency are allowed to 'survive', with further repetitions gradually producing models which always land planes safely.

Computer Spreadsheets

Computers are particularly useful for solving numerical problems, and carrying out numerical tasks, due to their speed, accuracy, ability to handle vast quantities of data, and the fact that, as far as we can tell, they don't get bored doing the same calculations day after day! When we use a computer to solve a problem or make a decision, the problem is normally expressed as a series of logical steps. Uncertainty can be allowed for by using such techniques as probability (as in the expected values approach to be covered in chapter 4) and random numbers, with the computer generating a random number which is used to represent a particular result occurring.

Random numbers are an important part of modelling mathematical decisions, the most famous illustration being that of Monte Carlo Simulation. Gamblers wishing to determine the best approach to take in particular situations can face a very large number of possible outcomes. It might take them a very long time, with the possibility of making mistakes, to calculate the exact probability of particular cards being dealt to them and the banker, then add together all possible outcomes to determine what they should do.

This repeated calculation of mathematical outcomes is an ideal situation for computers. The gambler can set up a model such that the computer generates random numbers, treats them as cards (e.g. 1 = ace of clubs, 2 = 2 of clubs, through to 52 = king of spades), and applies the rules of the game. This model can be run millions of times so that eventually the best strategy in any particular situation can be established. An ideal package for setting up such a model would be a computer spreadsheet.

In the dark ages (before computer spreadsheets were invented) when large numbers of figures had to be manipulated, such as in budget preparation, it was necessary to prepare sheets of analysis paper, with rows and columns representing different attributes and figures being entered in cells. Thus a column might be used for each month, a row for each type of expense, and April's wages figure entered in the cell where these two attributes met.

Major weaknesses existed with these manually prepared sheets:

- changing even a single entry might necessitate a large number of recalculations, each requiring erasure of the original figure and entry of the new one. To examine a range of scenarios (e.g. various inflation rates/sales figures etc.) would require a great deal of time and effort;

- deleting or inserting a row or column would leave the sheet looking untidy and often require complete redesign and recalculation of the whole sheet;

- to facilitate changes, sheets were often completed in pencil, which could result in figures becoming unreadable due to fading over time. Using pen and whiting out any errors or changes would be time consuming and messy, both methods requiring typing of the sheet once completed if quality presentation was desired;

- working papers were required to record the origin of each entry;

- identical entries, and identical calculations performed on a number of different figures, had to be individually performed and entered;

- extraction and presentation of figures was time consuming, particularly if required in the form of a graph or chart. Quality graphics were extremely difficult to achieve;

- due to the difficulty of making changes, an existing sheet could not easily be adapted for a new use;

- use of complex or advanced formulas would require great skill and effort on the part of the user, and perhaps the use of mathematical and financial tables;

- security could be a problem, with unauthorised changes being made.

Despite these weaknesses no better alternative existed so the use of analysis sheets was very common. Small wonder that a new means of carrying out numerical analysis which overcame the weaknesses of analysis sheets would prove extremely popular. Computer spreadsheets are here to stay!

Spreadsheets - What are They?

(Where have you been for the last 25 years?)

Spreadsheets are computerised analysis sheets. A grid of cells is available for the entry of text, numbers or formulae, and the computer makes all necessary calculations.

In most spreadsheet packages, columns are given letters and rows numbered so the cell in the 5th column and 10th row would be called E10. The cell in the 30th column, row 105 would be AD105. The full spreadsheet would normally contain hundreds of columns and thousands of rows, but individual applications, often called models, are best kept to a much smaller size otherwise they become unmanageable. It is very easy, however, to use the output from one sheet as input to another, so for example, one spreadsheet could be used to work out the total wages bill, and this figure carried to another sheet which works out total cost.

Formulae are used to define relationships between cells (a formula could be placed in cell B10 so that the figure in that cell would be double the figure in cell A10. The formula would be +A10*2, * being the symbol for multiplication) and / or to apply mathematical functions such as factorial, standard deviation or net present value.

It is often helpful to separate individual sheets into sections, thus the results, or output section, might be contained in a certain area, cells requiring input data kept in another, and intermediate calculations in a third. This makes data entry and reading of results much simpler than would be the case if these various elements were jumbled together all over the spreadsheet.

Advantages of Spreadsheets

Taking each of the weaknesses of manual calculations outlined above in turn:

- calculations are computerised and thus almost instantaneous, mistake free and effortless. This assumes that the designer of a particular sheet knows what he is doing. GIGO (Garbage In, Garbage Out) expresses the point that it is impossible for the computer to know that when you tell it to multiply by 5 you actually mean 5%. Many packages do automatically check for obvious mistakes such as 'formulae which refer to cells which are blank or contain text' and 'data not used by any formula in the model';

- entries can be changed by simply replacing old with new, and small changes to long entries can be made by editing. The formula +A10*B3*(D3:D12)*10% would mean 'take the value in cell A10, multiply it by the value in cell B3, and by the total value of all the cells in the range D3 to D12, and then by 10%'. If you wanted to change the percentage to 12%, you would enter the cell containing the formula and just change the 10 to 12. Recalculation is very fast and effortless, so examination of various scenarios (often termed 'what if' analysis)is facilitated, resulting in better information;

- deletion / insertion and even moving of rows and columns is simple, with formulae being automatically updated to refer to the new location of source cells (e.g. if column A was moved to become column K, a cell formula that had been +A3*10 would become +K3*10 automatically);

- changes replace the original cell entry, so no erasure is necessary. Printing is fast and can be done at any time with no manual typing required;

- the formula underlying each figure in the model is held by the package. It can be seen by either moving to the relevant cell or obtaining a cell contents printout;

- data can be taken directly from the model for graphical, chart or other presentation. In the case of integrated packages, spreadsheet data can be fed directly into other applications such as database or word processing;

- models can often be adapted to a new application. A couple of additional rows may enable a cash budget for one company to be used for others;

- mathematical and financial tables and formulae are built-in to spreadsheet packages. Those not built-in can be entered into relevant cells, the copy facility being particularly useful for formulae based on arithmetic or geometric progression as is the case with many financial formulae. An arithmetic progression is one where a constant amount of change takes place e.g. £10 more every month, and a geometric progression is one where the rate of change is constant, e.g. 10% more every month.

   If each month's sales were expected to be 5% more than the previous month's, the first month's sales being in cell C5, the required formula in D5 would be +C5*105% (or +C5*1.05). Copying that into adjacent columns would result in automatic updating of the reference cell so that cell K5 would contain the formula +J5*105%.

   It is possible to override this automatic updating of references if it is not desired. Many packages require the insertion of a $ sign before any element of a formula which is not to be updated, so if we had wanted all the cells in the adjacent columns to refer back to cell C5, the formula copied from D5 would have had to be +$C5*105%.

- access to models can be restricted by use of passwords. It is also possible to 'write protect' cells so that the formulae or other information contained within cannot be accidentally overwritten.

To illustrate practical use of a spreadsheet, consider the following situation.

Sandy's Winner

Your friend Sandy has been telling you how well her business is doing. "I am on to a winner! Look at my unit costs:

	£
Metal Man Kit	5
My workers for assembling the kits	3
Total	8
I sell the assembled men to Tough Toys for	10
So I make a profit per man of	2

Now Tough Toys want to increase their order, starting in May, from the existing 8,000 units per month to 20,000 per month.

That means I make £40,000 profit per month!

I will need a van to cope with the increased workload, but it will only cost £20,000 and that is only 2 week's profit. Even you will agree I can start planning that dream holiday, why at this rate I could buy a new car......bigger house......always wanted a boat......"

All this talk of profit and no mention of cash flow had left you a bit concerned, so you asked a few questions:

Question	Sandy's Answer
Do you pay cash for the kits and worker's wages?	Yes
Do Tough Toys pay you cash on delivery?	No, 1 month later
How much stock do you keep?	Enough for 1 month's sales
How much cash will you have at the end of February?	About £4,000.

You decide to calculate Sandy's predicted cash flows for the months of April to August inclusive, and think about steps Sandy might consider to cope with any cash flow problems she might run into.

The answer is shown on SANDY'S SPREADSHEET, which is repeated showing the formulae contained within the cells. Explanation follows, but if you happen to have convenient access to a spreadsheet package, it would be extremely good practice for you to set up a model of this problem.

Sandy's Spreadsheet

Base Data

	A	B	C	D	E	F	G	H	I	J	K
2		£					£000				
3											
4	Kit	5		Van			10				
5	Wages	3									
6	Sell price	10		Opening Cash			4				
7											
8			Feb	Mar	Apr	May	Jun	Jul	Aug	Sep	Oct
9	Sold Units in 000		8	8	8	20	20	20	20	20	20
12	**Intermediate Calculations**										
13	Bought Units in 000		8	8	20	20	20	20	20	20	
16	**Answer**										
		Cash Budget for April to September. All in £000									
				Mar	Apr	May	Jun	Jul	Aug	Sep	
20	**Receipts**										
21	Tough Toys			80	80	80	200	200	200	200	
22											
23	**Payments**										
24	Van					20					
25	Kits			40	100	100	100	100	100	100	
26	Workers			24	60	60	60	60	60	60	
27			Total	64	160	180	160	160	160	160	
28	Net Cash Flow			16	-80	-100	40	40	40	40	
29	Opening Cash Balance			4	20	-60	-160	-120	-80	-40	
30	Closing Cash Balance			20	-60	-160	-120	-80	-40	0	

Sandy's Spreadsheet – Formulae in cells

Base Data

	A	B	C	D	E	F	G	H	I	J	K
2		£					£000				
3											
4	Kit	5		Van			10				
5	Wages	3									
6	Sell price	10		Opening Cash			4				
7											
8			Feb	Mar	Apr	May	Jun	Jul	Aug	Sep	Oct
9	Sold Units in 000		8	8	8	20	20	20	20	20	20
12	**Intermediate Calculations**										
13	Bought Units in 000		=+D9	=+E9	=+F9	=+G9	=+H9	=+I9	=+J9	=+K9	
16	**Answer**										
	Cash Budget for April to September. All in £000										
				Mar	Apr	May	Jun	Jul	Aug	Sep	
20	**Receipts**										
21	Tough Toys			=+C9*$B6	=+D9*$B6	=+E9*$B6	=+F9*$B6	=+G9*$B6	=+H9*$B6	=+I9*$B6	
22											
23	**Payments**										
24	Van					20					
25	Kits			=+D13*$B4	=+E13*$B4	=+F13*$B4	=+G13*$B4	=+H13*$B4	=+I13*$B4	=+J13*$B4	
26	Workers			=+D13*$B5	=+E13*$B5	=+F13*$B5	=+G13*$B5	=+H13*$B5	=+I13*$B5	=+J13*$B5	
27			Total	=SUM(D24:D26)	=SUM(E24:E26)	=SUM(F24:F26)	=SUM(G24:G26)	=SUM(H24:H26)	=SUM(I24:I26)	=SUM(J24:J26)	
28	Net Cash Flow			=+D21-D27	=+E21-E27	=+F21-F27	=+G21-G27	=+H21-H27	=+I21-I27	=+J21-J27	
29	Opening Cash Balance			=+G6	=+D30	=+E30	=+F30	=+G30	=+H30	=+I30	
30	Closing Cash Balance			=+D28+D29	=+E28+E29	=+F28+F29	=+G28+G29	=+H28+H29	=+I28+I29	=+J28+J29	

Creation of the Spreadsheet

A column has been used for each month, and a row for each cash flow item and total. All base data has been entered in the first 9 rows, the only intermediate calculations are in row 13, and the answer is contained in rows 16 to 30.

For the intermediate calculation of monthly bought units in row 13, it has been assumed that each month Sandy buys the units to be sold the following month, so February's bought units are the sales in March. Thus, cell D13 contains the formula: +E9. Copying this into cells E13 to J13 resulted in the formula being automatically updated so that, for example the formula in E13 is +F9, which is what we want.

Row 21 contains the monthly sales receipts, again obtained by use of a formula. To obtain a particular month's sales receipts, we need to multiply the previous month's sales units (to allow for the one month credit given to Tough Toys) by the selling price per unit. Thus, cell D21 contains the formula for March sales receipts: +C9*$B6. The $ was included so that when this formula was copied into cells E21 to J21, to give the sales receipts for April to September, the selling price in cell B6 was used for each month. This contrasts with the C9 part of the formula, which does not contain a $ sign because we want to update the formula to refer to the next column's sales units each new month.

Similar approaches were used for the payments for the kits (cell E25 having the formula +E13*$B4) and wages (cell E26 formula: +E13*$B5).

Total payments in any month are those contained in the relevant column, rows 24 to 26. The formula =SUM(D24:D26) was placed in cell D27 and copied to cells E27 to J27, the formula being automatically updated.

Net cash flow is the difference between receipts and payments in any month (D28 has +D21-D27) and the closing cash balance is the opening cash balance, plus the net cash flow for the month (cell D30 has D28+D29). For all but the first month, the opening cash balance is the closing balance from the previous month (cell E29 has +D30). These formulae were copied across into the relevant cells for subsequent months. The opening cash balance for February was given in the base data, so was copied from the relevant cell (cell D29 has +G6).

Having designed the spreadsheet, presentation can be improved. In this case, the width of columns was adjusted to suit the size of figures and headings, headings were underlined and / or emboldened, and headings for individual columns were right justified to line up with the figures in the column. Grid lines have been included to make it easier to follow exactly which cell particular calculations are in, but could be removed if they were felt to detract from overall presentation.

Assumptions

Dealing with an artificial situation like this will always require assumptions to be made. In real life, it should be possible to establish the true position for many of them, although others may still have to be judged. In general, as any good accountant will tell you, assumptions should be pessimistic, so any surprises are nice ones!

'What if' analysis can be used to test the effects of changing one or more assumptions, or to show by how much particular figures can change before a certain result occurs, e.g. by how much sales can fall before an overdraft of over £100,000 is required.

Assumptions made in the spreadsheet answer include the following:

- sales will continue until at least October;
- the van is required as soon as sales increase i.e. in May;
- 'enough stock for 1 month's sales' means each month enough units are bought and converted to provide the units for sale in the next month;
- this means the higher wage level is payable from April onwards;
- Sandy's answers and all other information are correct;
- there are no van running costs, or other expenses (not very likely!)

The most dangerous assumptions are those we make without realising it. Am I guilty? Can you see any other implied assumptions which may not be valid, and could jeopardise the results?

What Sandy Could Do

Sandy has to cope with a £160,000 cash shortfall in May. Steps to deal with this, with their potential effects in May (check that you see how these are obtained) include:

- reduce stock e.g. to 1 week's sales. When monthly sales are 20,000 units, this represents 15,000 less units in stock, each of which would have cost £5 for the kit and £3 assembly wages. Thus payments would be reduced by:
  Kits £75,000;   Wages £45,000;   Total   £120,000
- delay paying suppliers e.g. for 1 month   £100,000
- insist on Tough Toys paying immediately   £200,000
- slow the rate of growth. Discussed below.

Most of these have possible adverse consequences e.g. Tough Toys are not going to be impressed with a demand for immediate payment when they are increasing their order so dramatically.

The best solution may well be to negotiate a temporary overdraft for at least 5 months. No interest rate was given, but a reasonable estimate of likely cost could be calculated. Even if interest was as high as 1% per month, it would only total (60+160+120+80+40)x £1000 x 1% = £4,600, which is relatively small given the figures in the answer.

Slowing the Rate of Growth

The root cause of Sandy's problems are the timing differences between her paying for kits and wages, and receiving money from sales.

In April, stock of assembled kits increases from 8,000 to 20,000 units, at a cost of £8 each, an increase from £64,000 to £160,000 = £96,000 extra tied-up in stock. Profit on 8,000 units at £2 each is £16,000, and is the only source of extra finance, leaving £80,000 to be taken from cash.

In May, debtors increase from £80,000 to £200,000 i.e. up £120,000. A van is also purchased for £20,000, so use of funds increases by £140,000. The only source of finance in May is profit on 20,000 units i.e. £40,000, hence the cash fall of £140,000 - £40,000 = £100,000.

From June onwards, there is no more increase in debtors, stock or any other use of funds, so the profit of £40,000 each month is all available to improve the cash position.

Slowing the rate of growth would slow the increase in stock and debtor levels, and therefore slow the increase in financing requirement. The effects can easily be determined by 'what if' analysis, in this case changing the monthly sales figures in cells F9 to K9. For example, growth at 1,000 units a month from May onwards would leave a positive cash balance at all times (£8,000 in May, which was the month with the worst cash shortfall in the original scenario).

It would also, however, reduce profit considerably, May having 11,000 units less sales, so £22,000 less profit. It would take 12 months to reach the proposed 20,000 units level, with a total loss of 66,000 sales, or £132,000 profit. One, or a combination of, the other options is clearly preferable, as can be seen by simply comparing the £132,000 lost profit to the possible interest payable on a temporary overdraft, calculated above as at most £4,600. (Another important consideration would be whether Tough Toys would be happy with such a slow growth rate - they may well look to another supplier, possibly taking all their custom there).

It is in the area of 'what if' analysis that the spreadsheet comes into its own. You may have thought that time spent designing the initial spreadsheet was greater than that required to calculate the answer manually. That may be true (presentation may not have been as high quality) but what if it was suddenly realised that, e.g. the cost of kits was going to be £6? Kit costs, total payments, net cash flow, opening, and closing balances would all have to be recalculated for each month, about 35 changes. On the spreadsheet, only cell B4 has to be changed, the computer updating all relevant cells, and quality printing being readily available (assuming you have a printer!)

In short, it can be said that spreadsheets are a dramatic improvement over manual analysis. Consequently their use has become extremely common in financial and other numerical analysis such as budgeting, ratio analysis, investment appraisal and mathematical modelling. They have simplified and revolutionised the ability of people to use fairly detailed calculations, and experiment, in their decision making.

This chapter has examined decision making, deciding between possible course of action. Chapter 4 considers risk management, recognition and dealing with potential problems, and completes consideration of the logical approach to problem solving.

Self Test Questions

3.1 How are raw score converted into weighted scores when analysing options numerically?

3.2 To what extent does weighting factors and giving raw scores to each option remove the subjectivity from decision making?

3.3 What is the probability of throwing a 6 on a dice?

3.4 If you have just thrown a 6, what is the probability of throwing another one next?

3.5 What is the probability of scoring 9 with 2 die?

3.6 What are the main advantages and disadvantages of using computer spreadsheets for numerical analysis?

Exercises

3.1 If you had 20 red balls and 2 white ones in a bag, what would be the probability of drawing all the red ones first?

3.2 4 adult tickets and 2 child ones for a coach trip cost £130, while 5 adult and 3 child ones cost £170. How much is each ticket?

3.3 If you have access to a spreadsheet package and would like to practice its use, you could attempt to set up models of some of the numerical illustrations in this book or any such analyses you have carried out manually. The weighted scores approach used at the beginning of this chapter for comparing various ski holiday options would be ideal.

Check that the model works, i.e. gives the same answers as obtained manually, then carry out 'what if' analysis by changing one or more of the variables. For example, in the ski holiday analysis, holiday 4 'won' with an overall 7.8, compared to holiday 4's total of 7.5. What if:
1. holiday 4 had only been given a raw score of 7 for location?
2. weighting of location had been only 0.2, with night life 0.4?

If you do not have access to a spreadsheet, analyse the changes manually.

One of the exercises at the end of chapter 4 is answered on a spreadsheet. You may wish to use that for further practice.

Answers to Exercises

3.1 Probability of drawing all 20 red balls out first can be thought of the other way round: what would be the probability of the last 2 in the bag both being white?

Any of the 22 balls could be last, and that could be either of the white ones, so the probability of the last one being white is $2/22$.

Given that one of the white balls is to be last, probability of the other one being next to last is $1/21$.

Applying the multiplication rule, the probability of both events occurring is:

$$2/22 \times 1/21 = 2/462 = 1/231$$

This is the same answer as given by the longer version, which determines the probability of each ball drawn being red:

$$\frac{20 \times 19 \times 18 \times 17 \times 16 \times 15 \times 14 \times 13 \times 12 \times 11 \times 10 \times 9 \times 8 \times 7 \times 6 \times 5 \times 4 \times 3 \times 2 \times 1}{22 \times 21 \times 20 \times 19 \times 18 \times 17 \times 16 \times 15 \times 14 \times 13 \times 12 \times 11 \times 10 \times 9 \times 8 \times 7 \times 6 \times 5 \times 4 \times 3}$$

By inspection, you can see that the only differences between top and bottom of this long fraction are the factors in the short version. All the others cancel each other out.

Using the formula from the chapter $^{[r!(n-r)!]}/_{n!}$ would give $^{(2! \times 20!)}/_{22!}$ for either approach, again simplifying to $2/(22 \times 21)$ and thence $1/231$.

3.2 4 adult tickets and 2 child ones for a coach trip cost £130, while 5 adult and 3 child ones cost £170. How much is each ticket?

Expressing the problem mathematically:
$4A + 2C = 130$ formula 1
$5A + 3C = 170$ formula 2

In the correct solution, the values of A and C must be the same, so these two equations will be simultaneous. Using the first approach covered in the chapter, formula 1 can be rearranged:

$4A = 130 - 2C$
$A = (130 - 2C)/4$

Substituting this into the other formula:

$5[(130 - 2C)/4] + 3C = 170$

Opening the brackets:

$162.5 - 2.5C + 3C = 170$
$0.5C = 7.5$
$C = 15$

Substituting this into one of the original formulae:

$4A + (2 \times 15)$	$= 130$
$4A + 30$	$= 130$
$4A$	$= 100$
A	$= 25$

Checking the results in both original formulas:

$(4 \times 25) + (2 \times 15) = 130$ correct total cost for formula 1
$(5 \times 25) + (3 \times 15) = 170$ and for formula 2

Turning to the simultaneous equations approach:

$4A + 2C = 130$ formula 1
$5A + 3C = 170$ formula 2

Multiplying formula 1 by 5, and formula 2 by 4 will give the same number of As in each new formula (multiplying by 3 and 2 respectively would have given the same number of Bs, and worked equally well):

20A + 10C = 650 new 1
20A + 12C = 680 new 2

Taking new 1 from new 2:

2C = 30
C = 15

Finishing off as for the other method, that is by substituting C=15 into any of the formulas to determine the value of A, then checking the result (C=15, A=25) by confirming it gives the correct total cost for each of the original formulae.

3.3 If holiday 4 had only been given a raw score of 7 for location, its weighted score for that factor would have fallen to 7x0.4 = 2.8, a reduction of 0.4 (which could have been calculated as 1x0.4, i.e. the reduction in the raw score x the factor weighting). Total weighted score for holiday 4 would have fallen to 7.4, so holiday 1 would now 'win'. This reflects how tempting and easy it is to 'fiddle' the results to give your favoured option the highest total weighting.

If weighting of location had been only 0.2, with night life 0.4, holiday 1's total weighted result would be unaltered since it had a raw score of 7 for both those factors. Holiday 4 had raw scores of 8 for location and 6 for night life, so its weighted score for those two factors would change:
Location was   0.4x8 = 3.2, now 0.2x8 = 1.6, down by 1.6
Night life was 0.2x6 = 1.2, now 0.4x6 = 2.4, up by   1.2
Net effect   down by 0.4

Holiday 1 wins again. Fiddle!

Chapter 4
Risk Management

Heads I win, tails you lose.

That would certainly be ideal risk management from my viewpoint.

Individuals and organisations are increasingly recognising the need to manage the risks they face. This partly reflects acceptance of historical failure to do so effectively, but also that pace of change and complexity of modern life is so great that reacting to events is unlikely to prove a successful strategy. Events can have such devastating consequences that no matter how good ones decision making technique, a workable solution cannot be found.

Risk management does not necessarily mean risk avoidance. Most activities involve some level of risk, and we would not want to exclude them all from out repertoire. Consequently, risk management is often aimed at lessening the likelihood of adverse events occurring, lessening their consequences, or passing them on to other parties.

Risks faced by individuals in their private lives include:
- being involved in a major accident;
- a house fire;
- getting pregnant (I am not personally worried about that one!);
- health;
- being made redundant.

Organisations have some similar concerns, but also:
- loss of a major customer or supplier;
- new competitors;
- shortage of resources e.g. materials / staff / equipment / finance;
- bad debts;
- economic changes (interest / exchange rates, economic downturn).

115

Appreciation / Specification

In recent years, there has been an increase in concern over the governance of large organisations, much of this being centred on a feeling that such organisations have failed to identify, assess and guard against major risks faced by the organisation. Directors of private companies are now required to conduct annual reviews of the effectiveness of internal financial, operational and compliance controls and systems, and risk management.

In the NHS, Clinical Governance has become a major issue, defined by Professor Liam Donaldson, Chief Medical Officer, as "A framework through which NHS organisations are accountable for continually improving the quality of their services and safeguarding high standards of care by creating an environment in which excellence in clinical care will flourish". NHS bodies are required to provide evidence that they are managing themselves so as to protect patients, staff, the public and other stakeholders against risks of all kinds.

Avoidable adverse events (i.e. where errors in procedures or treatment have been made) are thought to cost the NHS over £3 billion p.a. Many of these events are repetitions of previous failures. One of the roles of the recently created Commission for Health Improvement (initially abbreviated to CHIMP, but presumably due to adverse comments by staff, now called CHI) is to carry out Clinical Governance reviews. This includes investigation into persistent clinical problems and annual publication of a performance assessment framework.

In the risk analysis phase of risk management, we are trying to identify events that would have a major adverse effect if they took place. Clearly this is much broader than solving a well-defined problem. Approaches commonly used to ensure all risks are considered include consideration of past events, round table discussion, strategic risk reviews, specific analysis of particular areas of concern, interviewing staff and customers, and completion of checklists and questionnaires. Much of this relates to the Learn stage of problem solving, helping to highlight the iterative and cyclical nature of the whole process.

This analysis is frequently summarised on a grid measuring likelihood (or probability) and consequences of particular events. Thus an individual might analyse their risk profile as shown in diagram 4.1.

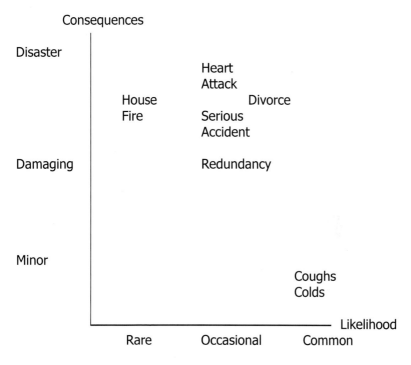

Diagram 4.1 Possible Risk Profile of an Individual

Deciding the probability and severity of particular events, and thus their position on the grid, is very difficult. This should not be taken as a serious weakness in this process, however, since the grid is meant to be indicative and not an absolute and precise statement of the risks faced by an individual / organisation. The real purpose of attempting to plot risks on the grid is that it encourages thinking about, and investigation into, the risks faced. It often also leads to recognition of risks hitherto missed.

Once approximate positions on the grid have been decided, attempts can be made to move risks towards the bottom left, by reducing their likelihood or severity, thereby reducing their effect.

Use diagrams 4.2 and 4.3 to analyse your own risk profile, and that of your organisation. I hope you do not discover anything that is a common disaster!

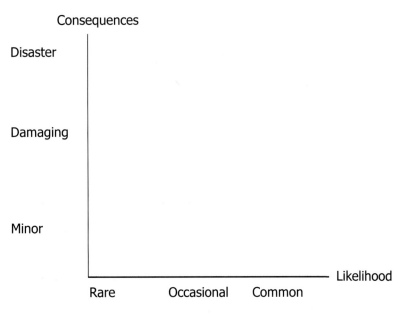

Diagram 4.2 Your Personal Risk Profile

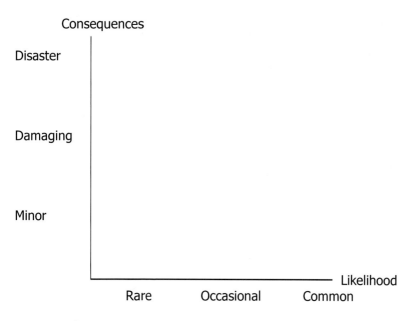

Diagram 4.3 Your Organisation's Risk Profile

Expected Value

A numerical approach to identifying and quantifying risk is that of using probability, and the concept of expected value.

By analysing the results (value or cost) of particular outcomes, we can establish the level of risk faced by an organisation taking a particular decision which has various possible outcomes. If we can determine the probability of each outcome, we can work out the weighted average value or cost of taking the decision, by multiplying each result by its probability, and adding these together. This weighted average result is known as the expected value, often abbreviated to EV. (When considering risk, the outcomes will normally be costs, so we could refer to expected cost, but most people would still use the term EV, showing it as negative).

The arithmetic is very similar to that used in chapter 3 when deciding where to go skiing. Each factor was given a weight to reflect its importance, then each solution was given a raw score under each factor to reflect how well it achieved that requirement. Multiplying the raw scores by the weights, then adding the results, gave a weighted score for how well each solution achieved the overall objectives. We could have called this the expected value of each solution.

To illustrate calculation of expected value, consider a person who wants to estimate her average weekly income. She usually works for 5 days a week, earning £100 a day, but 10% of the time she does an extra day paid at 'time and a half', and 30% of the time she only works for 4 days.

Multiplying the value of each outcome by its probability, we have:

Days worked	value £	Probability	Expected value £
4	400	0.3	120
5	500	0.6	300
6	650	0.1	65
Overall EV			485

Note that the probability of a 5 day week was assumed to be 60% since the other two outcomes accounted for the other 40%, and overall probabilities must total 1, or 100%. Thus possibilities such as her only working for 3 or less days, or being ill all week, have been ignored. In a real situation, such possibilities should be considered and allowed for, and would in fact represent the worst risk situation.

EV represents the average income she would receive each week over a long period. Her actual earnings in any particular week would be £400, £500, or £650 depending on which outcome actually occurred that week. On no occasion would she receive exactly £485.

EVs in Risk Analysis

Expected values are particularly useful when faced with choosing between a number of possible actions, each of which has a number of possible results. We can calculate the EV of each action, then choose the one with the highest EV.

To illustrate, suppose you were planning a trip to London by train, but had the possibility that a friend might bring you back by car. You must decide whether to buy a single or return ticket.

Before making the decision, you would have to obtain the relevant information. Assume this to be:
- Probability of lift   0.8
- Cost of tickets
    - Single   £20
    - return   £26

Now the EV of each option can be calculated. Before reading my answers, see if you can work them out below.

Option 1: Buy a Single Ticket

Outcome	Cost	Probability	Expected Value
Lift	£20	0.8	£16
No lift	£40	0.2	£ 8
Overall EV (cost)			£24

Option 2: Buy a Return Ticket

Outcome	Cost	Probability	Expected Value
Lift	£26	0.8	£20.80
No lift	£26	0.2	£ 5.20
Overall EV (cost)			£26.00

Note that in this simple situation, the costs for the second option were £26 whether or not a lift was received, so it was not really necessary to calculate it for each outcome and sum the results.

Option 1 had an EV of £24, and option 2 an EV of £26. This indicates that buying the single ticket would result in the lowest average cost if the decision were repeated many times. In practice, however, many people would take the return ticket option, based on such arguments as:

- their worst position would be a cost of £26, compared to a possible £40 under the single ticket option;
- they would only 'lose' £6 if the 'wrong' outcome occurred, whereas under the single ticket option they would 'lose' £14 if the lift appeared;
- they believe in 'Sod's Law', that whichever option they go for, the 'losing' one will occur (i.e. the lift will not show up) so going for the one which costs least if things go 'wrong' is a good idea (this approach ignores the probabilities, just making the decision based on 'worst outcome');
- they would know precisely what their costs would be, thereby helping plan their finances for the day;
- if they buy the return ticket but get a lift, they will still be happy to have met their friend and have a comfortable trip home chatting about their holidays. If, on the other hand, they buy a single and the lift does not happen, they will be really annoyed at having to buy another ticket and travel home alone.

Risk Management

In chapter 2 I promised that in chapter 4 I would consider whether entering the national lottery is a rational thing to do, so here goes.

On EV grounds, based on your chances of winning a prize, it would definitely not be rational to enter since only 25% of the stake money is returned as prizes. Does that mean there are millions of people in the country acting irrationally?

I am tempted to say 'Yes, it probably does' but in reality there are many reasons why someone might enter the lottery perfectly rationally despite the poor odds of winning:

- they will not miss the £1 stake, but if they happen to get a big win, it would completely change their lives;
- it gives them a dream;
- the excitement gained from watching the draw is worth 75p (the difference between the £1 paid to enter and the 25p EV of winning);
- their friends all enter, and they want to be part of the group, particularly as they couldn't stand being the only one not to win if the syndicate is lucky;
- they are happy for half the money staked to go to charities;
- they have not calculated the odds, and / or do not understand them, being either unable or unwilling to do so.

When attempting to manage risk, and particularly to calculate EVs, it is necessary to decide the probability of particular outcomes. To conclude this section on expected value, I will briefly consider ways in which this can be done. Before reading on, can you think of, say four?

My four ideas are:
1. Use statistical analysis to work out the precise probabilities. This only applies to those situations where all possible outcomes are known, along with their individual probabilities, good illustrations being most casino and card games. Where there are several events to be considered, it may be necessary to use probability rules such as the multiplication and addition rules, and know when they apply! Alternatively, a spreadsheet model of the situation could be set up, using the computer to generate random numbers;

2. Analysis of past events, and the frequency of particular outcomes. If keen to establish the likelihood of your car engine lasting for another 20,000 miles, it may be possible to obtain information about general longevity of that particular model;

3. Specific in-depth analysis of the situation under consideration. Could you carry out an inspection of your car engine to assess actual wear and tear?

4. Ask an expert. If keen to know whether the snake that just bit you was poisonous, and what are your chances of survival, see if you can recognise it in a book, on a website, or describe it to a person at the local poisonous reptiles advice centre.

Causes
Having considered ways of Appreciating and Specifying risks, we can move on to the later stages of the problem solving model, starting with Causes.

For each identified risk, it is necessary to think about what circumstances could cause it to occur. This will lead into the Solutions stage, discussed below, in which one approach to risk management will be to reduce the likelihood of the circumstances occurring. (Can you think of any other approaches?)

Because each risk is different, it is impossible for me to suggest all possible causes. Instead, I will briefly consider some major risk areas, highlighting common causes.

House fires are commonly started by **individuals being stupid or careless**. This includes falling asleep while smoking in bed, hanging clothes over or close to an open fire to dry, or leaving fires unattended. Severity is increased if flammable materials are around, internal fire doors have been left open, and there are **no** smoke **alarms** or **automatic** sprinklers. Many deaths result from the fact that the people in the house do not wake up, being overcome by fumes in their sleep. Fires in public places can result in death or severe injury due to **poor escape routes** or **bad signage**.

Heart attacks are, as far as I am aware, most common in **unfit, overweight, highly-stressed** men. The fact that I don't really know is a sign of **ignorance** on my part, which is very common too. (No, I meant many people don't know, not that I am ignorant about lots of things!) I have a pet theory that they often occur following a large meal, when a person tries to sleep on a very full stomach. **Sudden extreme** exercise, such as running for a bus or playing squash for the first time in years, is also a possible cause.

Many accidents are caused by drivers' **excess speed, not adjusting to changing conditions, dangerous actions, poor communication, invalid assumptions** as to what other drivers will do, or **mechanical breakdown**. Others result from poor road maintenance, layout or lighting, coupled with insufficient warning signs;

In many cases, an adverse event results from **a combination of a number of factors all going 'wrong'** at the same time, contrasting with the 'weakest link' idea covered in chapter 2, which looked at situations caused by an **individual weakness in a system**.

The Escaping Prisoner model of accident causation depicts potential accidents as prisoners trying to escape, and each of the factors as a part of the security system aimed at keeping them in. A person trying to prevent accidents occurring is viewed as the prison systems designer, trying to ensure there are no **breaches in security**. Each factor can be considered in turn to look for possible weaknesses and ways to prevent them occurring, and the whole system can be reviewed to check for circumstances in which the 'wrong' combination of events could occur.

Psychology is extremely important in the process of risk management, as illustrated by the following considerations.

Many people tend to think **disasters happen to other people** so **fail to guard** fully against them. Much criticism is targeted at smokers, because they **know the risks** involved, **but still** smoke. Some people go as far as to claim that smokers should not be treated for lung cancer because it is their own fault. Interestingly, similar arguments are rarely heard against obese people who suffer heart attacks having over eaten for years. Note that I am not a smoker, but do have a tendency towards rotundity.

Other people are '**doom mongers**' tending to overstate the likelihood and severity of particular events, possibly deliberately, but often due to their pessimistic outlook. Many people feel this is what happened with 'The Millennium Bug', with the **risk faced being vastly overstated** in both likelihood and severity. The problem here is that it encourages **over-reaction**, which is **poor risk management**.

This leads to another psychological issue, that of **people acting like lemmings**, and allowing themselves to be 'hyped up' into a communal **panic**. A good illustration of this was when there was a petrol shortage due to a blockade by farmers and haulage drivers - people queued for hours to top up their car, vastly adding to the shortage as the average content of a petrol tank rose from just over half full to virtually full. The next day, word got around that a petrol shortage would soon lead to a food shortage, so the supermarkets were cleaned out! The blockade was lifted after a few days, but then **rumours** went round that they were about to start again, and back out went all the drivers to queue.

An important issue resulting from the extensive use of e-mail, pagers and mobile phones, is the fact that rumours are very **quickly and easily circulated**. Individuals must try to act rationally and not allow themselves to be pulled along by the crowd. Excuse me a minute, just got to get some petrol……

Judging the validity of a particular action by the actual results, rather than the likelihood of success or failure, is another psychological problem. In the case of 'The Millennium Bug', a commonly held belief is that all the **money spent on preventing** an IT disaster was **wasted** because nothing untoward occurred. The fallacy here is that it assumes that the same result (i.e. nothing) would have happened without the preventative actions. Similar logic to that used by an elderly neighbour: "I shouldn't have had that anti-flu injection: I didn't catch it"!

Many managers **react adversely** to one of their **staff pointing out weaknesses in procedures**, to such an extent that 'whistleblowers' have to be given special guarantees of protection if they are to be encouraged to act. Again, if individuals believe their promotion prospects would be lessened if they publicised their own errors in the hope of avoiding repetition throughout the organisation, they are unlikely to do so. One way of dealing with both of these issues is to introduce confidential reporting procedures.

A final illustration of the importance of psychology: how would your partner react if you put 'divorce' down as minor /commonplace in your personal risk analysis grid?!

Psychological aspects of decision making are covered in more detail in chapter 5.

Solutions

By considering the axes of the analysis grid used in the earlier stages, 2 approaches are evident:
- lessen the likelihood of the event occurring;
- lessen the consequences if it does occur.

Lessening Likelihood

In the extreme, lessening the likelihood would be achieved by total avoidance of the activity leading to the risk:

Risk Management

- afraid of flying - don't fly! (Rather reminiscent of the person who went to the doctor's and said "My neck hurts when I do this" only to receive the response "Well, don't do it then!");
- when some schoolchildren were killed in a skiing accident, several Education Authorities banned all such trips.

Clearly this kind of approach does avoid the risk, the problem is that it also prevents the related activity taking place, and achievement of the related objectives. Very few activities involve no risk, so a person regularly following this approach would have so few things they could do they would achieve very little with their life, and risk (!) dying of boredom.

More often we are looking for ways to continue the activity but lessen the likelihood of undesirable events. This will follow naturally from the earlier identification of potential causes:

- avoid fires starting by teaching people to be more safety conscious, and ensuring highly flammable materials are not used in manufacture of clothing;
- reduce the chance of a heart attack by taking regular exercise, reducing stress level, and changing one's diet;
- prevent road accidents by improving road conditions (speed bumps, lower speed limits) and setting higher standards for acquisition and retention of driving licenses (ban people who drink and drive, break speed limits, or are not physically and mentally fit enough to drive safely. Treat road safety much more seriously).

The Escaping Prisoner model of accident causation was mentioned above, highlighting the need to consider each possible causal factor in turn to look for ways to prevent it occurring, and to review the whole system for circumstances in which the 'wrong' combination of events could occur.

Attempts should be made to ensure that weaknesses in one factor would not line up with those in other factors. Checks should be made as to each factor in the accident prevention 'security system', to ensure it is still operational and establish any incidences of failure. The best time to find out that your reserve parachute has been eaten by moths is not when your main chute has just become tangled!

Lessening Consequences

This approach accepts that accidents may happen, but attempts to minimise their effects. Consequences of an event can often be reduced by planning ahead and taking precautions:
- disaster plans and dry runs by emergency services;
- protect known high risk areas e.g. cover for vital staff / equipment, and regular backing up of computer records which accepts that computers do 'crash' from time to time, but most damage is caused by a failure to take basic precautions;
- insist on such safety measures as the wearing of seat-belts, and not allowing children under a certain size to occupy front seats, to reduce the effects of car accidents that do occur;
- reduce fire damage by fast action: fit heat detector alarms and automatic sprinklers, have plenty of fire-fighting equipment around, train staff to tackle small fires before they become big ones, ensure fire escapes exist and are unlocked, easily accessed, properly signed, and not blocked with piles of highly flammable paper.

A tragedy which occurred on a funicular ski lift, resulting in well over 100 deaths, sadly illustrated some of the above causes and potential solutions very well.

It seems that there was a general complacency with regard to the possibility of fire, with no automatic sprinklers or fire-fighting equipment on the train, little evidence of fire-fighting training of the staff, and no written instructions for passengers to follow. Little scenario analysis or planning had taken place such as to test what would happen if a fire did occur, and how to prevent it spreading and minimise its effects.

This complacency did not stop with the lift company. Some ski-wear is highly flammable, with the presumed assumption that, since it is worn in a very cold, barren environment, fire is not an issue. In practice, in addition to circumstances such as that being discussed, many people wear their anoraks in the evening when they go to pubs, restaurants and discos.

When the fire occurred, there was initial disbelief that it could have happened. Investigators just could not see how it had started, spread so quickly, and been so intense. At first, the assumption was that it must have been caused by grease and oil being set alight by sparks from a cable, but this did not seem to answer the question. Another theory was that some skiers had fireworks with them (to celebrate the start of another fabulous ski season) and somehow these were set off.

The train was in a tunnel which climbed steeply through the heart of the mountain. Unfortunately, when the fire started, the steep tunnel acted like a chimney, allowing the fire to suck air in from below, which supplied it with a vast amount of oxygen. It also allowed the fire to spread very rapidly up the carriages of the train, and toxic fumes to travel up the tunnel killing the driver of the train coming down and several people waiting at the top station.

Passengers found it extremely difficult to escape from the train, with no fire exits being provided. Those who managed to get off were unsure which way to go. The steepness and confined space made it extremely difficult for emergency personnel to gain access.

Discussion of such an event is extremely painful, and may seem to be attempting to blame individuals or score cheap points. That was certainly not my intention, which was to illustrate how, in an apparently secure environment, a tragedy can occur, and see if lessons could be learnt. I feel very deep sympathy for all those involved, particularly the staff who cannot be held to blame for what was clearly a completely unforeseen and tragic event.

I trust the above comments were read in that spirit.

Transferring the Risk

Having considered lessening the likelihood of a problem arising, and its consequences if it does, there is still another possible approach to consider: can the remaining consequences be passed on to another party? This can be achieved in a number of ways:

- careful wording of contracts including penalty clauses, guarantee and warranty periods, and get-out clauses in the event of, say war or strike action;
- insurance. This is particularly relevant for those risks in the top left quadrant of the analysis grid (rare, but disastrous) since the insurer is able to take on a large number of individual's risks, using the premiums to meet the costs of the few individuals who actually suffer the loss, a process known as spreading the risk.

For risks towards the bottom of the grid (i.e. relatively minor consequences), administration costs would be likely to exceed any benefit from insuring, while any risks towards the top right (common disasters) would either meet with point blank refusal from the insurance company, or attract such high premiums as to make the cost prohibitive.

Carrying the Risk

Whatever risks remain after the above solutions have been put in place, are carried by the individual / organisation, which means that they suffer the consequences of whatever events take place. This is, of course, irrespective of whether or not they were aware of the risk - unfortunately, the ostrich approach to risk management does not work. Many organisations have been ruined by an event they did not even perceive as a risk. This can be something as basic as their major customer changing their source of supply, or more dramatic such as deliberate sabotage by an employee. Entrance of new competitors, 'sudden' development of a vastly superior product (Dyson's vacuum cleaner design), or new methods of trading (the internet) are further examples. This is closely linked with the ideas of strategic management outlined in chapter 2.

Risk Management

The ostrich approach to risk management doesn't work.

Conclusion

The remaining stages of the ASK SIR L model, Implementation, Review and Learn are the same for risk management as for general problem solving, discussed in chapter 2.

Potential risks are virtually limitless, but it is hoped that the techniques covered in this chapter will help you avoid, and / or limit the consequences of the really nasty ones in your life.

Chapters 2 to 4 have discussed the logical approach to decision making. Chapter 5 considers the potential weaknesses of this approach, ways to deal with them, and an alternative approach to the whole issue: Magical Mind Games.

Self Test Questions

4.1 List 5 major risks faced by:
  i. individuals

ii. organisations

4.2 What attributes of risk are often measured on a grid?

4.3 What are the basic steps in calculating the EV of a decision?

4.4 How would you determine the probability of each outcome?

Exercises

4.1 What factors would you take into account when deciding whether to insure your car 'fully comprehensive'?

4.2 You are organising a conference on Wild Life on Mars, and must decide what size hall to book, small (100 seats), medium (200 seats) or large (400 seats). Cost of hire is £150, £350 or £450 respectively. Each person attending will pay £25, but cost you £3 for handouts and £12 for refreshments.

Experience tells you that demand is dependent on the weather, and you have decided the following figures are relevant:

Weather	Probability	Attendance
Hot	0.2	150
Average	0.7	80
Cold	0.1	350

In order to avoid disappointing people too much, anyone you are unable to accommodate will be sold a set of the handouts for £6.

Calculate the monetary value of each outcome, and the expected value of each of the 3 possible hall bookings.

Can you think of, say 6 other factors that should be borne in mind when making the decision?

Answers to Exercises

4.1 Factors to take into account when deciding whether to insure your car 'fully comprehensive':

Various types of accidents possible, their likelihood and consequences. How likely is it that they would be your fault? (Possible psychological factor here - we all tend to think that we are great drivers, and any accident would be someone else's fault). Even if not your fault, could you prove it? Would the other person admit it? Would they be insured?

Your driving record and experience, typical annual mileage, type of driving and conditions - high speed motorway, or short trips to the local shops? Age and value of your vehicle? How vital is having a car available to you - for work and leisure? Are alternative vehicles available? Are you the 'bread-winner' for a number of people?

What is the cost of various types of insurance, allowing for any no claims bonus available? Exactly what does each cover? Who is paying the bill? Does the difference in cost represent a sizeable portion of your net disposable income?

Does anyone else drive the vehicle, and would they contribute to the insurance cost?

4.2 (See Life on Mars spreadsheet)

Largest EV is given by the small hall option, so this would be chosen on purely short-term financial grounds. Other possible factors to bear in mind include:

With the small hall option, you would always earn at least £650, the others having minimum returns of £450 and £350, both occurring 70% of the time.

Life on Mars

Basic data

	Small	Medium	Large
capacity	100	200	400
hire fee	150	350	450
	Audience	**Extras**	
charge	25	6	
handouts	3	3	
refresh	12		
net	10	3	
Outcome	**Average**	**Hot**	**Cold**
Probability	0.7	0.2	0.1
Attendance	80	150	350

Intermediate Calculations

Hall Size	Small			Medium			Large		
Outcome	Ave	Hot	Cold	Ave	Hot	Cold	Ave	Hot	Cold
Demand	80	150	350	80	150	350	80	150	350
Attenders	80	100	100	80	150	200	80	150	350
Extras	0	50	250	0	0	150	0	0	0

Results

Hall Size	Small			Medium			Large		
Outcome	Ave	Hot	Cold	Ave	Hot	Cold	Ave	Hot	Cold
Net Income									
Attenders	800	1000	1000	800	1500	2000	800	1500	3500
Extras	0	150	750	0	0	450	0	0	0
Total	800	1150	1750	800	1500	2450	800	1500	3500
Hire fee	150	150	150	350	350	350	450	450	450
Profit	650	1000	1600	450	1150	2100	350	1050	3050
Probability	0.7	0.2	0.1	0.7	0.2	0.1	0.7	0.2	0.1
	455	200	160	315	230	210	245	210	305
Overall EV	815			755			760		

| Regrets | 0 | 150 | 1450 | 200 | 0 | 950 | 300 | 100 | 0 |

Revised Probabilities

Probability	0.5	0.3	0.2	0.5	0.3	0.2	0.5	0.3	0.2
Profit	650	1000	1600	450	1150	2100	350	1050	3050
	325	300	320	225	345	420	175	315	610
Overall EV	945			990			1100		

A rather strange decision rule which is often quoted in text books is that of 'Minimax Regret'. The 'regret' of a particular decision is its result compared to the best possible result you could have obtained for that outcome, calculated as follows. If you go for the small hall, but the result is high demand, you only earn £1600 when you could have earned £3050, so you might feel bad about 'losing' the £1450 difference. If you wanted to minimise the regret you could feel, you might go for the option with the lowest maximum regret. I have included a line of the spreadsheet showing the regret for each decision / outcome combination. Maximum regret for each decision is Small £1450, Medium £950, and Large £300. To minimise the potential regret, go for Large.

Turning to more straightforward points, you should consider psychological factors. Would you feel worse turning hundreds of people away from a small hall, or speaking to 80 people in a hall intended for 400? What impression would the various occupancy levels give your audience? If you hope to speak on similar subjects to similar audiences in future, are they likely to attend?

Perhaps you prefer the good old compromise approach: go for the middle size! At least it avoids the two extreme levels of mismatch between space available and take-up.

How sure are you of the accuracy of your predictions? There are two aspects to them: probability of particular weather, and resultant demand. Is heat the only relevant factor? What about rain? How hot is hot? It seems strange that attendance is lowest in average weather, somewhat better if it is hot, but very high in the cold.

I have included on the spreadsheet a 'what if' calculation for weather probabilities of hot 0.3, cold 0.2 and average 0.5. Hot would then have the highest EV at £1100, Medium next highest, £990, and Small worst at £945.

Chapter 5
Mind Games

MIND MORPHING ON THE FINE LINE

Mind Morphing on the fine line
Look OK and feeling fine
Thoughts collide escape my head
Awake, asleep, alive or dead
Freely dreaming loose control
Imagination starts to roll
Hearing light and seeing sound
Tumbling, twisting round and round
Climbing up but falling down
Crying laughs a smiling frown
Shouting tastes I never felt
Into another realm I melt

Mind morphing on the fine line
Looking rough, but feeling fine
Experiment with mental flow
Close to the line, I need to know
Where are the limits of this trip
How near the drop without the slip
How close madness, where's the edge
Genius fools on a mind leap's ledge?
Where the boundary to my thought?
Is random thinking dangerous sport?
Pain or pleasure, dark or light,
Pleasant dreams or nightmare fight?

Mind morphing on the fine line
Look like hell, but feeling fine
Fighting pressures to conform
Suppress my dreams and hit the norm
Taking time for thoughts to roam
Fear the fright of get back home
Might never find the flows again
To drift around a floating brain
Swimming pools of shining thought
Almost touched yet never caught
Don't want to chain or check the mind
Just set it free and drift behind

Mind morphing on the fine line
Total wreck, but feeling fine
Slow withdrawal from my jump
Then waking with a fearful dump
Turn back to face reality
"Want a fag or cup of tea?"
Pay the price and make a quid
Get a job, house, partner, kid
When they ask me what I've done
"Mucked" it up, or had my fun
Tell them I was feeling fine
Mind morphing on the fine line

As has been shown, the logical approach to problem solving is extremely effective in certain situations. There are, however, potential weaknesses and disadvantages with that approach, and in practice it is sometimes found that it does not seem to be working. This chapter considers how we can tackle these issues, and an approach I call Magical Mind Games which is often useful as either an alternative or supplement to the logical approach.

While Magical Mind Games is most effective if the mind is allowed freedom to roam, you probably won't want to go as far as implied in the above poem! (I would love someone to put it to music. Any suggestions? j.j.rayment@apu.ac.uk)

DISADVANTAGES OF THE LOGICAL APPROACH

The main strength of the logical approach is that it adopts a set of simple, progressive stages, based on the idea that, providing each stage is carried out correctly and completely, the answer will drop out in the final stage, and in most cases it does. Several weaknesses exist, however, and they are now considered under two headings, technical and behavioural.

Technical Weaknesses

Attempting to solve problems step by step has inherent weaknesses. Can you think of any? To start you off, I consider one, validity of the model, below. Don't turn the page without trying to think of some more.

Validity of the Model

Using a model as a framework for decision making relies on the validity of that model. Will working through its steps lead to implementation of a successful solution? Thinking of the model as a ladder, do the steps fit together, is it properly supported, and is it pointing to the right destination? If one of the rungs is weak or missing, the whole ladder cannot be trusted, and may be unsafe.

Do those using the model possess the required skills, or is it self explanatory and fool proof? Are the requirements of each step, assessment of its completion, the links between the steps, and precisely how one should move between them, clear? What should the user do if it proves impossible to complete one of the steps?

Whatever model is used, it is unlikely to be suitable for all decisions, so how should the correct model for a particular problem be selected?

Fragmentation

Adoption of a model may result in users only considering one step at a time, and not keeping the whole problem in mind. Because the steps build on, and rely on, each other, if any one step is not fully achieved (your foot misses the rung) it undermines the whole process, and could result in either complete collapse or a sideways slip. The latter may not be noticed by the person using the model (on the ladder), resulting in their continuing to climb, but arriving at the wrong destination. They may then attempt to implement a solution which would be obviously unworkable to anyone standing back and considering the whole.

Rigidity

In order to ensure the steps are easy to follow and end in the right place, individual steps and their inter-relationships must be clearly defined and targeted. This means once the user has started the first step of the model (set foot on the ladder) it is very difficult to change eventual destination. If the problem changes, it will be necessary to start from scratch: attempting to reposition a ladder while on it, or cross from one ladder to another, risks coming down to earth the hard way.

Assumptions

Over-reliance on 'the system' can lead to us not being sufficiently fundamental in our thinking, one common manifestation being a failure to challenge, or even recognise, the assumptions underlying our analysis. If these assumptions are not valid, any solutions resulting from the analysis are obviously of doubtful validity. Some examples of common assumptions which should be challenged are:

'A Car Can't Come Through That Gap!'

This clearly borrows heavily from the 'think once, think twice, think BIKE' advertising campaign of a few years ago, aimed at getting car drivers to remember that not everyone on the road is driving a car.

Mind Games

One of the most frightening moments in my life was the time I was doing about 50mph on my motorbike between two lines of stationary traffic. The driver of a car just in front of me suddenly opened his door, and I immediately realised there was no chance of stopping. I still vividly recall the slow motion vision I had of the bike smashing into the door and sending me flying through the air. Luckily, and presumably in blissful ignorance of my plight, he closed the door again and I flashed past with, no doubt, a very strange look on my face. For some reason shortly after that I decided to travel to work by train.

'If You Have a Health Problem, Go to the Doctor'

While that will often be the right thing to do, other possibilities should be considered.

For certain symptoms or circumstances, going to the doctor would be too slow. A man suffering 'indigestion and a tingling left arm' could be the start of a heart attack, and deciding to 'go to the doctor' in the morning could prove fatal.

For less serious conditions it will often be better to at least try to cure yourself, possibly with the advice of one of the agencies which exist to facilitate such an approach (NHS Direct, advice from pharmacists, internet self help groups). The fact that you are looking to cure yourself will encourage you to look for the causes of your symptoms. You know yourself far better than your doctor does, and can spend more time on the case! Running to the doctor for an instant fix at the slightest sign of illness can lead to over-reliance on pills and potions, and a general decline in one's immune system. Doctor's surgeries are notoriously dangerous places, so keeping away avoids the possibility of picking up some other, far nastier, illness in the surgery. ASK SIR L before the doctor!

'You Should Aim for the Top'

It is very easy to find yourself pushing for every opportunity for promotion without really thinking about whether it is likely to result in your achieving your long term life ambitions. Psychologically, it can be good to have targets to aim for, but if these are too high, constant failure may cause you to be dissatisfied with yourself. Promotion may bring more money, but also more pressure and stress, longer working hours, and entail moving to a new organisation, office and / or geographical location, including moving house.

This may have knock-on effects on personal relationships, with the cliché outcome that the individual achieves promotion, and obtains the extra money they wanted to be able to spend on their family, only to realise that they have found someone else to love them.

Very often, the drive for the top is based on another common doubtful assumption:

'You Will Live, in Good Health, for Many More Years'

I believe that it is psychologically very important for us to assume this to be the case, since any other assumption is likely to be very upsetting and lead to an excessively short-term attitude to life. Having said that, however, I must point out my concern, that if it is carried to an extreme, the assumption of long term-good health can encourage us to be too long term in our attitudes. Many people work for 40+ years building up a healthy pension with the dream that they can then spend their retirement travelling, walking, scuba diving, skiing... only to find that (assuming they get there!) by the time they retire they are too frail or unfit to partake in such activities. As with so many aspects of life, balance is required: live for today, but with an eye to the future.

'There is a Right Answer, Only One, and it Must Be Found Now'

A problem with the systematic approach is knowing when to move from one stage to another, for example, when to stop looking for solutions and move to selecting and implementing one of those already found. Some problems are insoluble, while others may have a number of equally valid solutions. Sometimes it will be impossible to tell whether particular solutions will in fact work until they are put into practice. It is often the case that the complete solution cannot be identified immediately, the correct approach being to implement a partial solution quickly, learn from the results, then build on it.

Have you any examples of assumptions that need challenging? This topic is returned to later in the chapter.

Methods

Another tendency in the area of not being sufficiently fundamental in our thinking is that we can become hooked on solutions that worked in other circumstances even though they may not be relevant in this case. My examples follow, but have you any of your own?

A karate expert might look to fight their way out of a situation where negotiation (or running!) might stand a better chance of success. That statement may, however, reveal an invalid assumption on my part, that karate experts are looking for a fight. In fact, part of martial arts training is aimed at early identification of potentially threatening situations and taking steps to avoid confrontation. Additionally, the self confidence given by their knowledge that they can take care of themselves often means such experts feel no need to prove themselves to others, so are more prepared to avoid conflict than many less self confident people. A friend of mine, a Tai Kwon Do expert, said that he is actually very keen not to use his knowledge / skill / power in anger because he is trained to always go for a combination of 'effective' hits rather than rely on one being decisive, so could severely injure or even kill an assailant. I tend not to jump out and go 'boo' when he is around!

Circumstances change over time, and it is important that we challenge historical solutions and approaches to ensure they are still valid in the modern environment. Business Process Re-engineering is a phrase used to depict the need to challenge current business methods to see whether better ones could be devised. Some examples of this are:

- replacement of metal by plastic in many products;
- use of minimal invasive techniques (micro-surgery, laser treatment, ultrasound) instead of such traditional approaches as major 'cold' surgery, to deal with a wide variety of health problems;
- moves toward internet shopping, and satellite and cable tv; and my favourite:
- the Russian eye surgeon who has his patients placed on a conveyor belt so that they can pass in front of him for their treatment.

Resource Requirements

A further technical problem with using a logical approach is that the time, effort, money and other resources required to carry out each stage may be either too great for the importance of the problem, or simply not available. Similarly, some of the stages in the process may not be necessary in that their output is either already known or would not alter the eventual decision. Again, if a solution is not ultimately found and implemented, all effort put into the early stages is fruitless (unless some Learning can be extracted). Any resources spent on unnecessary stages, excessively deep analysis, or unsolved problems, are wasted, so the logical approach can be inefficient.

Behavioural Weaknesses

When making decisions it is important to be aware of the human element of the process. This can be a particular problem when using the logical approach, but needs to be considered whatever approach is adopted. Chapter 6 considers group decision making in detail, but more general behavioural aspects are covered below.

Anticipation

I knew you were going to say that.

As discussed in chapter 2, when faced with a developing problem, the mind, using past experience, predicts and anticipates developments, then uses these predictions to plan its course of action. This helps us to react quickly but can have disastrous consequences, such as when a footballer commits themselves to a tackle, but the attacker taps the ball ahead and trips over the extended leg to 'win' a penalty.

An illustration often quoted as to the opposite extreme is that of the frog in boiling water! I do not know the original source (sauce?), but several management texts illustrate the need to be aware of changing environments by quoting the following 'fact'. A frog dropped into a pan of boiling water would soon hop out, but the same frog placed in cold water, which was slowly heated, would stay there until it died.

The moral of the story is supposed to be that the frog has very poor sensory devices / reasoning powers so does not realise the slowly changing environment is becoming hostile, or what is causing it. The same problem can apply to organisations: if they do not properly monitor their environments, they may be caught out by an accumulation of slow small changes. What I find slightly distasteful about it is (no, not the slowly cooked frogs legs!) the idea that someone has carried out such an experiment in the first place, then had the gall to publicise the results as though they were perfectly acceptable. My hope is that the whole thing is just a made-up, though still rather sick illustration aimed at getting a point across. My fear is that someone will try to replicate it with fluffy little bunny rabbits or ducklings (which reveals my prejudice against frogs), or me!

We are very adept at taking a few pieces of information and drawing inferences from them, which enables us to complete the picture. For example, how would you complete the following?

READY   STEADY   _____

Of course, fans of the TV show might say COOK, but in most circumstances, and particularly if I had started with the more professional TAKE YOUR MARKS, one would be expecting to be told to GO, either by word, whistle, flag or gun. Many are the times in which the word "STOP" has actually followed, but the competitors have still started the race, and real chaos can ensue if there is a long silence before any command is given.

This illustrates the fact that by starting to plan based on early information we sometimes allow it to have greater importance than information received later. Thus, sequence of arrival of pieces of information can affect our judgement of their relative importance. Many recruitment experts claim that interviewers often make subconscious decisions for or against candidates within the first 30 seconds of the interview, then cling to these opinions almost regardless of future events such as quality of response to questions.

Thus it can be seen that, while our ability to anticipate is very often advantageous, we need to be able to override it when necessary e.g. when it may lead us to make erroneous and damaging conclusions.

Artificial Boundaries

Sometimes we are so used to certain constraints being placed upon us that we assume them to apply when they are in fact not there. A phrase commonly used to illustrate this is 'boxed-in thinking', the solution being to 'think outside the box'. An example of this is the problem:

> "Can you plant four rose bushes so that they are all exactly 3 metres from each other?"
>
> Clearly a solution such as a square does not work since the diagonals are longer than sides.

Before reading on, think about the problem. You have been given a strong hint as to where the solution lies: what artificial boundary is preventing a solution being found?

Mind Games

When considering this problem, most people attempt to draw it on a piece of paper, but that may reinforce the artificial boundary! We are so used to planting things on flat surfaces, we automatically set that up as a subconscious constraint, and the paper is also two dimensional. Once the possibility of using 3 dimensions is recognised, most people can produce a solution fairly quickly. (If you have not solved it previously, have another go in the space below).

Three of the bushes must be positioned equally distant from each other, in a triangle. The fourth cannot be in the same plane as the other 3, so must be positioned in the centre of the triangle, sufficiently above or below the plane of the other 3 to form the required shape: a pyramid.

Once this is realised, any number of possible methods may be thought of for implementing the solution. Assuming three of the bushes to be on flat ground (they don't have to be) correct positioning of the fourth can be achieved by e.g. digging a hole, making a mound, or using a hanging basket.

Anyone who realised early on that the only way to have 4 items equidistant from each other would be to use a pyramid shape may have avoided being hung up on the 'flat surface' assumed constraint. This is a good example of the value of being able to look at problems from different viewpoints.

Planning versus Doing

Sometimes we accept a solution too easily: with more effort we could possibly find a better solution. In games such as chess, a better move might be found; more thought might lead to an improved house design.

Conversely, it is possible to spend too long planning instead of doing - a disease known as analysis paralysis:
    Q: Why don't planners look out of the window in the

"Right, I've worked it out: the guy in the white shorts should win."

morning?

A: Because they would have nothing to do in the afternoon! It is always possible to find an excuse for putting off a decision: waiting for more / better information / tests / consultation. This is particularly hard to resist when the decision or action is one that we do not like having to take, such as telling someone they are to be made redundant. In practice, the sooner you get it over with the better, since you are then able to forget about it and concentrate on the more pleasant aspects of life.

Another illustration of this is our daily 'to do' list. People often do the 'pleasant' things first (nice phone calls etc.), putting off the nasty ones. This means the whole day is spent worrying about the nasty things. By doing the nasty ones first, the whole day could be spent looking forward to the nice ones. It is also often true that the nasty ones are not so bad once actually tackled, so all that worry turns out to be 'wasted'.

I like the idea of wasted worry! Most often, there is no point worrying about something, so from that view point, all worry is waste, but the idea of 'wasted' worry could also be thought of as meaning we only have a certain amount of 'worry' available, so we shouldn't waste it! This could, in fact, be true: perhaps worrying leads to illness, and is actually bad for you. A slightly different angle on 'don't worry, be happy'.

Psychologically, we often feel good once we have tackled a problem, which is another reason for doing them early.

Bias / Prejudice

When I was a football referee, I knew I had had a good game when both teams thought I was biased against them. Can you recall anyone saying "We were extremely lucky to only lose 2-0, the decision to send off our goal keeper was entirely correct, and the centre-back should really have gone with him"?! More likely "Both their goals were off-side, one didn't even cross the line, the centre-forward dived, and we should have had two penalties!"

Each team's players and supporters are biased in favour of their own team, see things from their own perspective, and usually genuinely believe that most throw-ins should be theirs. In a match where each side were awarded 50% of the throw-ins, it is very likely that both would come off believing they were entitled to 60%, but were only given 40%.

We are all full of biases and prejudices. The most commonly mentioned ones are probably those involving our relationships with other people: race / religion / sex / age / height etc. These are considered later, but first I want to look at the possible bias we may have for or against particular approaches to problem solving. I can see that following the rose bushes example you want another chance to prove your mental dexterity, so here is an exercise for you to try:

A	A	A	B	68
C	B	B	C	73
A	D	D	D	76
B	D	A	C	?
67	78	73	71	

Each letter represents a number
Adding the letters in a column or row gives the end figure.
What is the missing number?

DO NOT READ FACING PAGE UNTIL YOU HAVE WORKED OUT THE ANSWER.

Letter Values

Those with a quantitative bias are likely to automatically look for a mathematical solution. Many people attempt to work out the value of each letter, possibly along the following lines:

Columns 2 and 3 both contain ABD, so the only difference between them is that column 2 then has a D, and column 3 an A. Since column 2 totals 5 more than column 3, D = A + 5.

Using that fact in row 3:   3D's + A = 76, so 4 D's = 81.   D = 20.25

(That isn't fair, I thought they would all be whole numbers!)

D = A + 5, so A must be 15.25.

Putting that in row 1 gives: 3x15.25 + B = 68
45.75 + B = 68
B = 22.25

In row 2, this gives: 2x22.25 + 2C = 73
44.5 + 2C = 73
2C = 28.5
C = 14.25

The letter values are A = 15.25, B = 22.25, C = 14.25 and D = 20.25

These could be confirmed by substituting the values for the letters in particular rows and columns.

The total for row 4 can now be obtained as
22.25 + 20.25 + 15.25 + 14.25 = 72

Equations

Another mathematical approach:

Column 1:   ACAB = 67
Column 3:   ABDA = 73

Removing AAB from each highlights the differences between the two columns. Column 1 totalled 6 less than column 3, so D = C + 6.

Column 2:   ABDD = 78
Row 4:   BDAC = ?

Row 4 has letters ABDC against column 2's ABDD, the difference being a C instead of a D. Since we know D = C + 6, row 4 = 78 — 6 = 72

While both the above approaches worked quite well in this case, a more difficult set of equations, or larger grid with more letters, would add complexity. The solver might not be lucky enough to hit on friendly equations that led to a quick solution.

Non-mathematical

Those less inclined towards quantitative techniques are more likely to look for other approaches, even if only out of desperation, so if you have been struggling with the maths, now is your chance! Such people may realise that they do not need to know anything about the letters in the grid (note that the second mathematical approach did not actually determine the value of every letter). The letters are deliberately being used in this illustration as a distraction, to tempt the solver to adopt the usual approach to this kind of problem: algebra. In fact, some people are so hooked on that kind of approach that they forget the actual question asked, instead focusing entirely on determining the value of each letter! If you allowed yourself to be so easily distracted, write 100 times **I MUST KEEP MY MIND SUPPLE.**

Thus non-mathematical people may really annoy their mathematical friends by coming to the fast, simple solution:

$$68 + 73 + 76 + ? = 67 + 78 + 73 + 71$$
$$217 \quad + ? = 289$$
$$? = 72$$

(Total for all 4 columns must equal total for all 4 rows (both equal the total value of all letters in the grid))

This approach works regardless of the number of rows / columns, and whether or not the individual letters represent whole numbers or difficult fractions.

Another illustration of using the obvious mathematical approach when a simple alternative exists was provided by the guide on a coach trip. Each time she wanted to know whether everyone was on board, she did a head count, on one occasion getting it wrong because she forgot to include herself! Eventually someone suggested the obvious solution to her (which was? Can you see a much better approach?).

Count the empty seats! It was a 56-seat coach, and there were 52 people, including her, on the trip. All she really needed to do was count 5 empty seats including her own.

Further Examples

Other forms of bias that we need to be aware of include our natural tendencies towards particular psychological traits such as optimism / pessimism, planning / doing, introversion / extroversion. I tend to:
- be over optimistic with regard the amount of work I can do, so take on too many tasks;
- spend too little time planning because I like to get on with the job;
- be naturally rather an introvert; and
- assume that I already know the best approach to a problem and don't need to consult others.

An interesting experiment (and far more acceptable than the 'frog in boiling water' one) is to write the words RED YELLOW BLUE on separate cards in the wrong colours and request your victims to call out the colour the word is written in as soon as they see it. Even though they are expecting a trick, when you turn over the card, most people call out the word, not the colour (e.g. a card with the word RED written in blue results in them calling out red. If they shout green, they may have a very odd form of colour blindness!) After a few goes, a slight change can be made by requesting the word, and not its colour, which may cause problems for those who were getting the colours right.

This experiment illustrates most people's bias in favour of the written word rather than colours, probably because they are so used to reading. Those more used to dealing with colours (e.g. artists) may reveal bias the other way.

Bias and Prejudice in Relationships

People often seem to be biased in favour of things that are like them. In the extreme, this may apply to those vegetarians who do not eat meat because they think it is wrong to eat animals: why is it OK to eat vegetables?! Do we really know that plants have no feelings? What agony is suffered by a carrot when it is dug up, skinned, boiled and eaten?

"Congratulations old boy, just right for the job."

As I said, that may be extreme, but the question is where to draw the line. Is it OK to eat seeds and nuts? vegetables? fish? chickens? cows? rabbits? wild animals? horses? pets? unknown people of a different race? anyone you don't know? anyone but family? not close family? your partner? yourself? In normal circumstances, you would presumably be willing to go part way down this list, then stop. I have tried to put it in the order in which I would become increasingly less likely to join the feast, which reveals some of my personal prejudices, but is my order the same as yours? Would circumstances change your position? In the film 'Alive!', which was based on fact, the survivors of a plane crash had to decide whether to eat the bodies of other passengers, and most did: would you? are you sure? how do you know?

Continuing with the idea that we are biased in favour of things which are like us, if that is true, does it follow that we would rather have relationships and dealings with people who are like us? I am English, male, white, mid 40's, fit and healthy, a lecturer, professionally qualified, incredibly intelligent, handsome, modest...... (As you read that list, what reactions did you have? Did any of your prejudices surface? Are any of mine revealed?). Does that mean I would have a tendency to socialise with / appoint / trust people like that?

Assuming bias to exist, important influences, as to the extent to which particular attributes affect our decisions, would be the relative importance placed on each attribute, and whether the bias changes depending on the circumstances and decision faced. Assuming I was biased towards people like me, would it be more important to me that they are of similar age, background or race? Sometimes certain attributes will be relevant to a decision, and if that is genuinely true, it is not bias if the factor is included: I might be looking for a dancing partner, and gender may be relevant. True bias is when I decide to give someone a bad mark in an examination because of the colour of their eyes!

One of the biggest problems with biases and prejudices is facing up to them, and admitting how biased we are. I regard myself as having very low levels of bias, but am I right? I like to meet and mix with people who are different to me because I often find them more interesting (oops, is that bias?!) This can be quite difficult to achieve because the places I frequent are full of people like me, so it becomes a bit of a 'chicken and egg' situation! People of my age who are fit and healthy are likely to spend quite a lot of their leisure time in a gym. Lecturers tend to be found in Universities, with professionally qualified ones teaching similar courses.

Being biased in our private lives would restrict our choice of friends and activities. If we only socialise with people like us, and read papers etc. targeted at them, we are in danger of only experiencing an extremely narrow band of behaviours and attitudes. We may never meet 'Mr Right' (no-one ever mentions the need to meet 'Miss Right', so I will continue the bias!) if he / she doesn't happen to be within the small section of society we are 'comfortable' with.

When I took up skiing, I visited Italy on several holidays, and realised that there are many aspects of Italian life-style that I rather admire. It was not until I lived in Australia for two years, however, that the extent of bias people can have against other people, and its stupidity and damaging effects, really came home to me. Many Australians had an incredible bias against English people, calling us "whinging poms" and cracking all sorts of pathetic insulting jokes about us:

> Q "What's the definition of good driving?"
> A "A busload of poms going over a cliff"
>
> Q "Where should you hide your money in England?"
> A "Under the soap"

Many of the joke tellers had been born in England, or at most were second generation Australians. This may cast doubt on my 'we like things like us' claim, or perhaps they are even more biased against people from other backgrounds. It is common to find rivalry and jealousy between groups of apparently very similar people (e.g. supporters of two football teams from the same city), possibly created as a psychological means of developing differences that don't really exist, so as to reinforce tribal feelings.

Being a fairly robust character, I was able to retaliate:

■ "When my great grandfather came to Australia, he only had 200 pounds -
    100 on each leg"

Q Customs Officer "Have you any criminal convictions?"
A Alien: "I didn't realise it was still a requirement"

Alien is the term used by both Australia and the US to refer to foreign entrants to their country, and tends to convey a modicum of prejudice. It does, however, conjure up some interesting images of the queue!

Other people would be tempted to berate the person telling the joke, only to be met with the retort "whinging pom"! This made me realise for the first time what it must be like for e.g. Irish people to be the constant butt of jokes such as:

"Paddy, I just saw a sign asking for tree fellers, if I get Mick to join us, shall we go for it?"

with the certain knowledge that if they complain they will be called 'miserable sods unable to take a joke'.

Most of the time, there is no real intention by the joke teller to offend the victim. The problem is that it does offend, and ultimately encourages genuine prejudices to develop. Many Australians were genuinely prejudiced, and even hostile, towards English people, which meant they were very slow to accept genuine attempts at friendship. Some of the people I eventually had very strong friendships with took a great deal of effort to bring round, but time is not always available for this, and why should it be necessary?

At work, any such prejudice is equally damaging. If we try to only appoint people like us, and only value such people's opinions, we are in danger of very narrow thinking, consideration of only a few aspects of a problem, and possible solutions, and not appointing the best person for the job. In the modern, rapidly changing, business environment, such an approach is doomed to failure since we wilhave second rate brains, applying the same old solutions to new problems.

For society as a whole, allowing such prejudices to flourish is extremely bad. Having been 'top dogs' since the industrial revolution, the English of the 19th and early 20th century are often portrayed as being incredibly arrogant, a very famous newspaper headline, of I believe the 1920's, stating "FOG IN THE CHANNEL - CONTINENT ISOLATED".

One consequence of such bias is that we tend to think of ourselves as superior to those we are biased against. The American Bill of Rights held certain truths to be self evident, among them being that all men are born equal (I don't know whether women existed in those days). Treatment of black and coloured people in the United States until very recent times (many would claim including the present) reveals the extent to which this 'truth' was believed by many Americans.

A couple of incredible points are the facts that "Red" Indians were officially excluded from the definition of men so did not have to be given any rights, and that blacks were defined as only equivalent to 2/3rds of a white when it came to voting rights!

As recently as the 1950s, Australian Aborigine children were often forcibly taken from their parents and placed in foster homes so that they could be given a 'good Christian upbringing', which was supposed to be better for them than staying with their 'ignorant' parents! Who was being ignorant?

In both the United States and Australia, in recent years, steps have been taken towards recognising the ignorance, prejudice, injustice and incredible arrogance of such actions. Attempts to make amends include returning land (as long as it isn't too fertile or rich in minerals etc.) to the small remnant of the aboriginal populations that have survived, and allowing them to take part in the opening ceremony of the Olympic Games.

Reading books about the treatment of such groups can be an extremely chastening, and frightening, experience. 'Bury My Heart At Wounded Knee' and 'How The West Was Lost' are two which reveal how incredibly brave, friendly and willing to share, native Americans were. Yet they were massacred, starved, swindled and cheated by the invading Europeans, who thought of them as savages, and the land as unoccupied and, therefore, free for the taking.

I said that these books make frightening reading for two reasons. Firstly, it is frightening to think that human beings can treat each other so incredibly badly, and I selfishly worry about what could happen to me if I was on the weak side in any such conflict. Secondly, I believe that there are other intelligent beings in the universe, and worry about how they might treat us if they ever came here.

The cases mentioned are only two of the many historical examples of racial prejudice, often backed by religious zeal, and invariably adopting a 'might is right' philosophy, which led to the world still being dominated by people of European descent. Treatment of the Irish, Scots, Welsh, Indians, Africans... by the English, Aztecs by the Spanish, and Jews by the Nazis are others. There are really no signs of such attitudes disappearing, as witnessed by recent turmoil throughout the world.

Such bigotry leads us to undervalue the people involved, and their opinions and strength, invariably to our cost. Both American Indians and Australian Aborigines held land to be sacred and not something to be owned and exploited; we knew better and are in danger of killing the whole planet!

Aztec and Mayan culture was extremely rich and varied, but the Spanish had guns, and a religious attitude which held all other religions and faiths in contempt. They conquered South America, stole all the gold and other riches, and obliterated anything to do with local civilisations, largely using religion as their justification. This has resulted in us still being ignorant of how the Mayan's developed, many years before we did, an incredibly complicated and accurate calendar that displays intimate knowledge of planetary and stellar movements.

The Allies adopted a Western approach in the Gulf War, focusing on destroying the other side's weapons and forcing withdrawal. Iraqi leadership seemed to all but ignore the fighting, concentrating on political / religious aspects instead. Ultimately, the Americans became so concerned about appearing to be the aggressor, that they ended the war very quickly and allowed sufficient of the Iraqi forces to survive for their leader to remain in power. Who won the war? (Who ever wins wars?!)

Ageism and Sexism

These are two forms of prejudice which have been to the fore in recent times, and the debate often reveals the participants' prejudices. It would be easy to write a book dedicated to either, and many people have, so I do not intend to cover them in depth here. Instead I will mention just a couple of aspects which I have found intriguing.

Until, say 10 years ago, it was often claimed that the English education system was biased in favour of boys, and that they tended to dominate classroom sessions, which was why they did better at school. Thus, it was desirable for girls to be taught separately from boys. Possibly as a result of publication and analysis of results 'league tables', it has been realised that girls now out-perform boys, and special consideration is being given as to how boys should be educated. Part of the problem may be reduced motivation resulting from a general loss of male self esteem, due to such factors as:
- years of relative decline in the number of traditionally male dominated jobs;
- less importance being placed, both in work and society, on possession of 'male' attributes;
- a constant 'drip, drip' of women's libbers undermining our frail egos!

Women had a legal retirement age of 60, and tended to live to 75, while men had to slave away at the coal face until they were 65, then dropped dead from sheer exhaustion at 67. This blatant prejudice is being partially rectified by moving the retirement age for women up to 65 in about 20 years time, but that will still leave women retired for 10 years compared to the men's two. Equity demands the lowering of the male retirement age by at least 5 years to 60. Join with me brothers!

In the workplace, many other attempts are being made to remove clear inequalities, including human rights legislation. This attempts to make it illegal to do anything that treats particular groups differently from others. It includes such hidden prejudice as only advertising vacancies in publications that are mainly read by certain groups. It will be interesting to see whether insurance companies which currently offer lower rates to certain driver categories will be allowed to continue to do so. One advertises for female drivers, including the statement that women drivers are better, surely a blatantly biased claim!

A particular problem with prejudice is that it is so ingrained that we do it without realising. An example of this is the fact that tall people tend to do well at interviews (possibly one of the few advantages us poor men still have - we are still generally taller than women, aren't we?) One explanation is that we tend naturally to respect and, literally and metaphorically, look up to, people who are taller. This possibly originated at a time when height tended to reflect physical power, and such power mattered.

Limited Attention Span

If you found your mind wandering during any of the above passages where I was getting some of my pet views off my chest, it could reflect another behavioural problem with decision making: limited attention span. (No, it could not be anything to do with the quality and content of what you were reading, so don't even think it!)

Once we have struggled with a problem for a while, we tend to get bored with it. This can lead to giving up (either formally, or just 'putting it to one side'), accepting the first solution which comes to us without properly thinking it through, or missing vital pieces of analysis.

Tackling These Disadvantages

The very act of recognising that the logical approach to decision making has disadvantages sets us on the way to tackling them, thus, if we suspect ourselves of being guilty of analysis paralysis we can take such steps as:

- placing a time limit on our planning. In chess competitions, there are time limits set for each player to make a given number of moves - an extreme version of this being lightning chess in which each player has only 5 minutes to make all their moves in the game.

- deliberately involving people who are action-biased in their decision making process with the hope that we will counterbalance each other's extremes.

Given my tendency towards optimism with regard to the amount of work I can do, insufficient planning, and failure to consult others, I should make conscious efforts to restrict the number of tasks I have in hand, ensure I plan them fully, and consult other people about them. The problem is that I tend to be over-optimistic......!

A further consideration when trying to improve our all-round decision making capabilities is the subject matter of the author's book Mind Management, aimed at showing how the strength, stamina and suppleness of the mind can and should be developed.

It is generally accepted that the body needs training and exercise to function efficiently and cope with difficult tasks, for example, successful running of a marathon requires months of slow building up of physical stamina. Many people, however, do not even consider the possibility that the mind might benefit from similar training and exercise.

Mind Management: "He stuck in his thumb, and pulled out a plum..."

They assume, for example, that they will be able to tackle a series of 3-hour examinations at the end of a course of study, without building up their mental stamina. Similarly, they assume they will be able to tackle complex problems without developing their mental suppleness and strength, starting with simple tasks. Contrast this with the way in which weight-lifters develop muscle and technique over many years before reaching their peak.

MAGICAL MIND GAMES

Most disadvantages of the logical approach stem from its encouragement of rigid / inflexible decision making. As has been alluded to throughout this book, Magical Mind Games is the phrase I use for those techniques aimed at overcoming these disadvantages by keeping our mind and thought processes supple, then using this suppleness when solving problems. Physically, unless we regularly stretch our bodies, they become stiff (can you still touch your toes and stand on your hands?) and I believe this applies to the mind.

The strength, stamina and suppleness of the mind can and should be developed.

When we have a nice, logical, 'straight line' problem, we can ASK SIR L to solve it, and provided he has a nice solid, unmoving target to go for, he can charge up to it, and often knock it down. He does however, have great difficulty in reacting to a changed target, turning round for another go if he misses first time, and using a different kind of attack. The problem with SIR L is that he is rather dated, slow and inflexible.

What we often need in the modern, light, fast changing, full of surprises world is a decision making approach to match. One well known tale begins "I opened the lid of the dustbin and looked out", the end of the sentence being so unexpected as to temporarily throw us off balance. Careful, SIR L, you might fall off your horse, and getting back on would be a real problem!

We need to be light on our feet, flexible, adaptable, and able to break out of the mind's traditional thought processes and patterns, challenge assumptions about a problem and consider it from new angles. SIR L can't really help us here: what we need is Little Ms Majik!

She is not weighed down by tradition, forced to follow straight lines, unable to move due to analysis paralysis, or to see the whole picture due to restricted view through the slits in a visor. She can duck and dive, dodge and wriggle, she can see ahead, fly and dream, she can wave her wand and solve things as if by magic! She is wonderful, and I love her!

Of course, sometimes she misses something obvious that good old SIR L would have easily picked up, or rushes into a solution without properly understanding all the issues involved, but I forgive her. She is much more fun than SIR L! Let's have some fun with Little Ms Majik!

Flexible Thinking

Much of the Mind Games approach comes from the concept of flexible thinking, which includes the idea of playing with different elements or facets of a problem instead of attempting to solve it by a logical step by step approach. Here we are looking for new thought processes and patterns, challenging assumptions, and considering the problem from new angles.

Mind Games

An earlier paragraph asked whether you can still touch your toes and stand on your hands, and you may have instinctively thought 'No'. Little Ms Majik knows, however, that even if they are not physically very flexible, with a little flexible thinking the vast majority of people will realise they can touch their toes - how else would they get their socks on? - and stand on their hands - even if they do leave a footprint on them!

LMM (as she likes to be called) wants to see if you can think flexibly by solving the following puzzle. Don't let her down!

Without taking your pen off the paper, can you join the nine dots with 4 straight lines:

This is a very well known problem, often used to demonstrate flexible thinking. It has any number of possible solutions, but I have only ever seen one 'in print'. Can you find 3?

Practice here or on any handy scrap of paper, but don't turn the page until you have come up with at least one solution, or put some real effort into doing so!

```
    *   *   *     *   *   *     *   *   *

    *   *   *     *   *   *     *   *   *

    *   *   *     *   *   *     *   *   *



    *   *   *     *   *   *     *   *   *

    *   *   *     *   *   *     *   *   *

    *   *   *     *   *   *     *   *   *
```

One solution is to realise that the lines are allowed to protrude beyond the boundaries of the square formed by the dots:

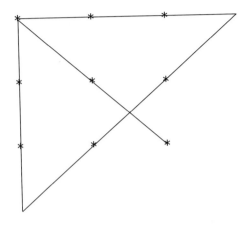

This is the solution that is invariably quoted, with the commentary that it illustrates our tendency, when attempting to solve a problem, to set our own artificial constraints which make finding a solution more difficult. In this case, the square of dots is often, wrongly, treated as a boundary on where the lines can go. Such artificial constraints are very often entirely subconscious, so before challenging them, we have to realise that we are unwittingly adopting them. Once the possibility of continuing the lines beyond the artificial constraint is pointed out to people, most solve the problem fairly quickly.

A commonly used phrase - thinking outside the box - refers to the ability to think about problems from new angles and without being restricted by invalid assumptions.

Before reading on, and particularly if you did not come up with any solutions, or you knew the above solution already and didn't really think afresh, see if you can come up with any other ideas. Try to really stretch your imagination, and have fun.

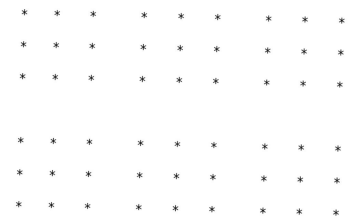

A second solution is to use 4 lines in the shape of a star or an E, achieved by tracing back over one or more lines:

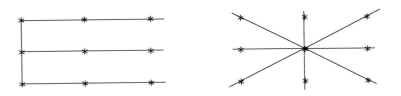

Some people would not accept these as valid solutions, arguing that, in the E case for example, there are 6 lines, not 4. The question was, however, deliberately loosely worded so that this solution could be valid in that we finish with only 4 lines even though 5 direction changes have been made. The idea of problems like this is to challenge the assumed "rules" and limitations placed on us not by the problem, but by our approach to it.

With a real problem, the validity of a solution depends on whether it solves the problem. For example, if the real problem here was to connect 9 points to a water supply using the minimum amount of pipe-work, the E solution would be valid and superior to the other 2.

Another solution would be to use a number of straight lines connected by curved ones (the question didn't say anything about not using curved lines!):

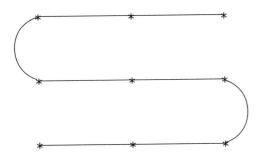

Again, many people would cry foul, but this could be a great solution if our real problem is a lack of straight pipes! It could be argued that the solution is still invalid because it only uses 3 straight lines and the question stated 4! We could cover this by either treating one of the lines as being 2 short lines, or by swapping one curve with a straight!

My favourite solution, partly because it displays the challenging approach I have been suggesting, but mainly because it appeals to my warped sense of humour, is to join all the dots with just one line — a thick one! Again, this might seem to be 'silly' but may be valid for certain practical versions of the problem: it is the 'shot gun' approach: make sure you hit the target by hitting everything.

Flexible thinking often helps to identify the crucial issues quickly, refocuses and refreshes the mind, or just frees it from an unseen block. The solution to the tennis tournament problem in chapter 1 (how many games for 1001 players?) illustrated this: instead of calculating the number of games directly, we can restate the problem as 'How many losers will there be?' As soon as this is done, the solution is obvious.

When we move from a particular part of a problem to consider a different part, our mind will still be subconsciously working on the original unsolved part, and often come up with the solution. Most people have experienced the situation where they have puzzled over a problem for hours only to have the solution come to them while watching television or walking the dog. This is one reason why I like to go on courses fairly regularly.

Golf courses, that is.

In general, the mind can be kept supple by deliberately tackling a wide variety of challenges and problems using different techniques, particularly those we do not naturally prefer. Often the person who would most benefit from tackling a particular type of problem or using a different approach is the very person who tends to avoid it! Computers and calculators hold some people in such a position and my experience is that once people confront their mental block they actually enjoy the challenge, find it easier than they expected, and gain immense satisfaction from their new found skills.

Specific Mind Games techniques include generation of alternatives, challenging assumptions, suspending judgement, problem reversal, dominant ideas, and crucial factors. The need to challenge assumptions has been covered previously, but Little Ms Majik has more illustrations of that and the others to show you!

Generation of Alternatives

It is tempting to stop looking for alternative approaches as soon as we find one that looks promising. It is also tempting to follow the same old solutions to new problems. For these reasons, it can be desirable for us to force ourselves to keep searching out alternatives, and to deliberately attempt to be creative in our solutions.

The game of chess illustrates this very well, and helps develop one's ability to generate alternatives, and decide when to call a halt. In the middle of a typical game, the players will be seeking ways of breaking through their opponent's defences or capturing some of their pieces, while at the same time protecting their own. Each player may have 30 possible moves, but only, say 5 of them, may seem to be worthy of much thought. The main difficulty comes with the fact that the player is not only thinking about the next move, but the continuation of the game from then on.

Good players will be looking for combinations of moves, and particular positions or patterns in their play that they know from experience tend to result positively. The complexity of the game means they will become used to dealing with a large number of calculations and factors at once, and generating logical strategies and plans. Experience will strengthen their awareness of circumstances in which great thought pays dividends, and how far ahead it is necessary to think in particular positions. All of these aspects help with generation and consideration of alternatives when faced with other types of problem.

One weakness with using games like chess to develop our thinking is that the rules of the game do not change. With real world problems, circumstances are constantly changing, so a solution which worked last time may no longer be valid, and conversely, one which failed before may be exactly what we are looking for now.

Setting a quota of approaches or solutions to be produced is a useful way of forcing consideration of a variety of approaches. I did this with the nine dots puzzle above, when I asked you to find three solutions. Many people know the 'standard' solution, and if pressed to come up with others initially resist the idea. Once they commit themselves to it, however, they often become very innovative in their solutions, thereby helping break away from ingrained rigidity. I hope you come under the latter category.

Little Ms Majik loves solving cryptic crossword puzzles, partly for the innate pleasure, but also because they are a good way of keeping the mind flexible. They encourage adoption of a wide range of ideas and alternatives in that they use a wide variety of ways of thinking about words and phrases rather than the obvious ones. Examples include:

Clue:	Ham set changed for a river (6)
Answer:	Thames
Logic:	HAM SET is changed i.e. the letters rearranged to give the anagram Thames (which you probably know is a river)
Clue:	GSGE (9,4)
Answer:	Scrambled Eggs
Logic:	GSGE is an anagram of eggs, i.e. gsge is the word eggs scrambled

Word searches and logic puzzles are also available to stretch the mind, a variation being where the clue consists of a few words which the solver is meant to interpret into a well known phrase or saying.

Clue:	look uleap (4,6,3,4)
Answer:	Look before you leap
Clue:	moon the (4,3,4)
Answer:	Over the moon

Creativity can be encouraged in a number of ways:
- use different analogies. Organisations are often described in army language: fighting with competitors, chain of command. Changing this to, say, flying, might encourage a fresh approach: following the wind, avoiding storms, coming out of the sun. I have used climbing a ladder as an analogy of decision making, can you think of others?;

- involve children or people with different backgrounds, to come up with completely new ideas, or make challenging statements which insiders may feel unable to;

- adopt role-plays or acting;

- deliberately adopt an unconventional approach, such as widen the problem instead of attempting to narrow it down;

- use mental imagery and maps, such as visualisation of 'success'. It is often claimed that weak golfers tend to play their ball into lakes and other hazards so frequently because they worry about doing so. This conjures up a mental image of that event occurring, and 'in she goes'. Instead, they should do what the strong players will be doing: focus on where a good shot would land;

- group approaches such as brainstorming are covered in chapter 6.

Challenging Assumptions

If we are making invalid assumptions about a problem, we are unlikely to solve it. We need to challenge all such assumptions to ensure their validity. This was mentioned earlier in the chapter as a potential weakness of the step by step approach to problem solving. This section looks at illustrations of this technique in action.

Is It Full?

A well-known illustration of basic time management skills challenges the assumption of when a jar is full!

The presenter produces a large glass jar and 'fills' it with pebbles, then asks the group:

"Is it full?"

Assuming Little Ms Majik is not around, the most common answer is "yes", whereupon the presenter produces some gravel and pours it in, shaking the jar so that some gravel works its way into gaps between the pebbles.

"Is it full?"

Most people will have cottoned on to the situation, and start to challenge the assumption, so will be looking for reasons to say "No". Sure enough, the presenter produces some sand (obviously unless it is Little Ms Majik doing the presentation, these props must have been prepared beforehand!) and pours some into the gaps between pebbles and gravel.

"Is it full?"

Everyone will now be in full assumption challenging mode by now, so call out "No" even if they can't see how anything else could be squeezed in! So as not to disappoint, the presenter pours some water into the jar, and asks the group:

"What is the moral of this story?"

How would you reply?

Given that the presentation is about time management, the obvious moral is that we can always squeeze more into a tight schedule. While this might be true, it misses the real point and hoped for lesson, which is not apparent until we think a bit more about what the gravel, pebbles, sand and water are meant to represent.

They represent the tasks and activities that fill our lives. Small pieces of 'gravel, sand and water' will always work their way into our schedule if we allow them to, and leave no room for the big things (pebbles) which are really important. In order to get those in, we have to put them in first. Imagine how difficult it would be to get the pebbles in if the water, sand and gravel had been in the jar already.

This book is not about time management (it would be much shorter) so turning to my point:

What assumption was challenged? 'When was the jar full?'

So when was the jar full? 'When the water was added'

Is that right?

It depends what you mean by full!

The jar was always full - initially full of air, which was gradually replaced by pebbles, gravel, sand and water. By the end, it is full of a mixture of all five. If we were only interested in pebble insertion, it would be fair to say the jar was full after stage one. The whole illustration is really based on an illusion - that the jar was empty in the first place. It depends what you mean by empty! At the start of this illustration I said 'assuming Little Ms Majik is not around, the normal answer is "yes"'. Perhaps she would also have said yes, but for different reasons!

Water Ways

Motorboats use propellers. Recently a new idea has been tested using a wave motion instead, based on the thought that fish use that approach, and nature's solutions are often best.

I Saw A Mouse

How many years is it since computer mice appeared? (Is the plural of computer mouse computer mice? It seems wrong, but so does computer mouses!)

Initially, one could make nervous types jump by shouting "Look, a mouse", and for about a year after that get away with any number of weak jokes about very long tails, pressing its ears, did it squeak, hard cheese if you lose it, have you seen a mouse dropping... (reminds me of the joke about the lady going into a shop to ask if they had anything for getting rid of mice:
Assistant: "Only this paste for blocking their holes"
Lady: "If I could get that close, I would tread on them!")

Now, if you shout "Did you see that mouse?" across the room, it is highly likely that everyone will assume you are talking about the latest 'Metal Mickey'.

Chess

Everyone knows two things about chess:
If you get your pawn to the other end, it becomes a Queen;
The fastest checkmate is by white, in four moves.

Neither is true! Do you know, or can you work out, the right answers?

If you get your pawn to the other end, it can become a Queen, but it doesn't have to. The rules allow you to chose which piece you want it to become (apart from two - can you deduce which?) Sometimes (admittedly, rarely) it is advantageous to opt for a knight, due to its unique move format which may give a vital 'check', or bishop or rook so as to avoid 'stalemate'.

I hope you were able to deduce that the two pieces you cannot opt for are a pawn or King, because either would just be silly. Take my word for it.

Black can 'checkmate' in two moves. White must have played the pawns in front of the Bishop and Knight on the King's side out of the way, so that when Black, having moved the King's pawn first move, moves the Queen diagonally to the Rook's file 'checkmate' results. (Those chess players among you will be able to annotate the moves for yourselves, I am sure).

Weighty Problem

You have a pair of scales. How many weights would be needed to weigh objects of any number of kilos from 1 to 40?

(I hope you are attempting these before reading the answers).

You might have thought along the lines that you need a 1kg weight, then a 2kg one, which together will give 3kg too, so the next weight needed will be 4kg. They can cope with up to 7kg, so next is 8kg. A pattern is revealed, with the next requirement being 16kg, then 32kg. Various combinations will allow all required individual values. Your answer would then be 1,2,4,8,16,32 i.e. 6 weights.

This approach suffers from the artificial 'assumption' that weights can only be placed on one side of the scale. As soon as it is realised that they can be placed on either side, it can be seen that weights such as 2 kilos could be dealt with by placing 1kg on one side and 3kgs on the other. A little further thought on these lines should enable you to come up with the correct solution.

Four weights are needed (1, 3, 9 and 27 kilos).

If You Had the Right 5th Weight, How High Could You Go?

Using similar logic to the previous answer should enable you to come up with the next weight being 81 (the next step up the 'power of 3' table) and the highest weight this would enable you to weigh would be the sum of all the weights you have, 121 kilos.

Problem Reversal

Sometimes the way to solve a problem is to look at it from another angle. Driving through Wales one day, I came round a corner to find the road blocked by a flock of sheep. I was very concerned that I would injure one of them, or they might damage the car, so how was I to drive past? The farmer had obviously read this book (!) because he reversed the problem and drove the sheep past me!

Many tricks are variations on the idea of looking at things from a different angle or meaning. One I fell for recently was when a friend asked me to "pick a card". She then told me to return it to the pack, carried out some elaborate shuffles, and started to deal the cards, including my selection, onto the table.

Soon she paused, took hold of the next card and said "I bet you £10 the next card I turn over will be yours". Betting is a mug's game, and I felt obliged to teach her this lesson by accepting the wager.

She let go of the next card, reached into the pile on the table and turned over my card. This taught me the lesson, betting is a mug's game!!!

Some of my favourite jokes are also based on looking at things differently:

Child: Mum, there's a man at the door with a bill
Mum: Don't be daft, it must be a duck with a hat on

Why has an elephant got 4 feet?
Because it would look silly with 6 inches!

(I have always assumed this must have a double entendre aspect, even though I first read it on the stick of a lolly aimed at young children. I assume the person authorising it either did not see the other meaning, or thought that anyone understanding it would be doubly amused, those not doing so would just have to make do with the simple version. Thinking of lollies reminds me of the time I was queuing for an ice-cream when a girl in the queue asked her father "Dad, can I have a Funny Face?" Her father was an expert in timing, so waited about 5 seconds for the tension to build, then gave us all the great pleasure of the obvious reply: "You've already got one, darling").

Patient: Doctor, I keep thinking I'm a pair of curtains
Doctor: Pull yourself together, man

OK, so I have a mental age of seven: it helps keep my mind young and supple! Anyway, I am certainly not the only one: when my father started his first job, the foreman sent him to the stores for a "long weight". After an hour or so, they thought he had "weighted" long enough.

Dominant Idea

Sometimes we are prevented from solving a problem because we allow ourselves to be put off by a particular approach to solving it. Until we can free ourselves from its influence, it keeps getting in our way, preventing clear thought about other approaches. This is closely linked to 'challenging assumptions', but I feel deserves attention in its own right.

The tennis tournament problem in chapter 1 was a good example, with the tendency for us to focus on the number of rounds to be played, as was the number puzzle earlier in this chapter, with its temptation to use a formula approach.

People wanting to lose weight often assume that to do so they must eat less. This encourages them to spend most of their time thinking about food, and invariably means they permanently feel hungry. Not surprisingly, this combination usually results in loss of willpower, and an eating binge which replaces any lost weight with a vengeance.

Try an alternative approach: what about eating more?! Stuff yourself full of good things to feel permanently smug tummied and leave no room for the bad. Further illustrations follow.

Fit for the Future

Due to my propensity to rotundity (get fat easily) and dedication to culinary delights (eat too much of the bad things just mentioned) I undertake vast amounts of exercise in order to maintain my Greek God appearance. When I first started attending gyms, they were full of fit young men in serious training, either to build stamina for sports such as football, or the 'muscle brigade' pumping iron to develop beefcake. The instructors were all superb specimens who seemed to sneer at anyone slightly out of condition.

The dominant idea was clearly that gyms were for the dedicated fitness fanatic. Most women, and the men who would have benefited most from attending, were put off, so the potential to provide wide ranging health improvements to the general population was not being achieved. This basic attitude also applied in schools with fitness sessions (PE and games) clearly focusing on those already fit, particularly if good at team sports.

Over the years, the scene changed dramatically. More attention was given by doctors and people in general to the need to keep fit, particularly giving the heart regular aerobic exercise. Resistance machines, which did not require the user to replace the heavy weights used by some muscle mountain with their puny little ones thereby revealing their relative weakness, were introduced. Rooms were kept bright and fresh, instead of filled with the stale smell of sweaty bodies, and video monitors introduced, showing music videos and television programmes. Aerobics studios were introduced in which 'step' and other classes were held. Aerobic machines were given pride of place, with weights relegated to the side lines. Many schools entered into arrangements with local fitness centres (a more user-friendly name) to allow their pupils who were not keen on team sports to attend sessions at special rates.

Even with the above changes, however, the dominant idea still seemed to be that fitness centres were for the young. More recently, this is being challenged, with emphasis being placed on the benefits of exercise for the middle aged and elderly. Aerobic exercise helps keep the heart and lungs working efficiently, but equal importance is being given to the role of weight-lifting in maintaining bone density and helping keep osteoporosis at bay. Ways are being sought to break down the psychological barriers that many older people find in attending such places. A particularly successful approach is that of having older trainers, with whom such users tend to feel more relaxed.

Whose Side Are You On?

A dominant idea in British politics has been: are you on the Left or Right, with strength of opinion and attitude spoken of as being close to the centre or far out.

Such terminology has been used to define people's political persuasion for many years, yet does not really reflect the modern political scene. Labour has been thought of as Left, and Conservative as Right, but New Labour seems to be happy to adopt many traditionally Conservative ideas such as privatising London Underground and Air Traffic Control, and has built up a very large budget surplus by restricting public spending. It seems loath to tax the rich highly, and I find it virtually impossible to distinguish between the economic policies of the two major parties. Liberal Democrats are now the 'spendthrifts', promising increased taxation of the rich to pay for it.

Aside from the narrowing of differences between the parties, the idea that a simple term such as 'left' could cope with the complexities of modern politics is absurd. To my mind, all of the main parties view the 'big' issues from the same side, or have no firm commitment or policy on them. Examples include abortion, prejudice, global warming, euthanasia, attitude to Europe and the Euro, Northern Ireland, Scottish, Welsh and English regional devolution, direct versus indirect tax (e.g. tax on petrol), and spending on and basic attitude towards education and health. It is very difficult to place these issues as left or right, and it seems that where there are different approaches available, differences of opinion exist within the main parties to a far greater extent than between them.

Perhaps it is time for a completely fresh approach in British politics, say a more inclusive coalition style, more referenda, and separation of economics from other issues. Basic attitudes may need expressing in new terms such as 'hard' or 'soft', or as different positions in a triangle, circle or cube. It is difficult to see how such change would occur with the two party system entrenched and supported by ingrained party loyalties and the 'first past the post' voting system. Perhaps it will require a crisis to force it through, or perhaps I am guilty of assuming the status quo, and the political scene will in fact change dramatically and easily in the new environment of the 21st century.

Crucial Factors

Very often, the solution to a problem will revolve around solving one or more particular difficulties. The most important step here is to identify what these factors are. Once that is done, approaches to their solution can be agreed, possibilities including concentrating exclusively on finding a direct solution for that factor, trying to redefine or reposition the problem so that the factor no longer applies, looking for general solutions which would take account of the factor automatically, and temporarily ignoring it completely to see what solutions can be found to the rest of the problem.

Getting Hung-up

Consider the following scenario. You force your way into a room through the door which was bolted from the inside, and is the only way into or out of the room. There is nothing in the room other than a dead man, hanging by his neck on a rope, his feet dangling about a foot (30 cm) above the floor, which is covered by a large pool of water. **What happened?**

What is the crucial factor, which must be solved in order to solve the whole mystery?

The man had committed suicide by hanging himself, but **how did he get himself and the noose high enough with no chair to stand on?**

The clue is the pool of water.

He stood on a block of ice, which has now melted.

I believe there is a detective story which revolves around a similar puzzle, except that time a person had been stabbed but there was no weapon apart from a pool of water.... Another interesting variation was the film in which the murderess cooked dinner for the detectives, using the, now thawed, side of beef murder weapon!

Light Fantastic

A recent example of challenging a long held assumption (and you know what I think of those!) because it did not fit with a crucial factor is that of speculation as to the speed of light. Everyone knows that the speed of light is constant, at around 186,000 miles a second, Einstein having used this basic 'fact' in his analysis of the universe and his theory of relativity. Anyone challenging this idea would be holding themselves open to ridicule, yet it did not seem to be capable of explaining, or even being consistent with, several crucial cosmological facts such as the size, mass and age of the universe.

Two cosmologists recognised that such blatant inconsistencies could not just be ignored, so they thought around the problem to see exactly where the inconsistencies were, and what would be required in a solution that did fit with all known facts. They new that the speed of light is constant, but their calculations showed a much faster speed was required to be consistent with calculations relating to the early stages in the life of the universe. Then came the brilliant and fascinating new idea: at any moment in time, the speed of light could be a universal constant, but that universal speed could be changing over time. Thus, it may have been much faster when the universe was young, and slowing down ever since. Having come up with this idea, they then tested it to see if it really did fit the particular problem they were dealing with, and whether there were any other facts which it did not fit with.

My interest here is not in whether or not the speed of light actually is changing over time (though that is clearly very interesting in its own right). It is in the thought processes which enabled those involved to recognise a crucial weakness in existing theory, think around the problem facing them, challenge a basic accepted 'fact', find another way of looking at the whole issue, and generate a new solution. To me, this is a magic example of mind games.

Wired Up

Keeping to the light theme, imagine you are faced with three light switches you know operate three lights in another room, but you don't know which switch is which. You only have one chance to go into the other room, and it is not possible to see into it from outside. How could you solve the problem unaided?

The crucial factor is that there are three lights and switches, but only two conditions for the circuits: on or off. Turning either one or two on would allow identification of the odd one out, but the two circuits in the same condition would still be problematical.

So, how do we get round the crucial factor? Big hint: the first sentence in the preceding paragraph contained an apparently obviously valid assumption!

There are, in fact, more than two conditions for each circuit! The crucial third condition is 'recently switched off'! But how does that help?

A recently switched off light bulb is hot. All you have to do is label the swicthes, say A, B, C. Turn switches A and B on, wait a while, then switch A off. In the room, the light which is on relates to switch B, the bulb which is off but warm relates to A, and the off and cold one relates to C.

Suspending Judgement

When generating alternative approaches to solving a problem, it is tempting for us to reject ideas which seem to have a basic weakness, without properly considering them. This can be a particular concern if we are dealing with areas in which we may not have the requisite skills or knowledge to make a valid judgement. Pace of change and development in the modern world is such that this kind of situation may become increasingly common. We must look for ways of ensuring we include all possible solutions until they have been properly thought through and tested by suitably qualified individuals or groups.

The Hole Truth

An illustration of this idea is that of using a bucket with a hole in it to fetch some water. The immediate temptation might be to reject the bucket completely, but further consideration might reveal possibilities. Block the hole, get the water in a plastic bag using the bucket to support it to prevent it splitting, use the bucket but run between the water source and place it is to be used so at least some water is left, and so on.

Many very good and imaginative solutions to problems result from the ability to suspend judgement, very often because other people faced with the same problem have, whether consciously or subconsciously, rejected such solutions.

Careful Drivers

Road junctions at which 2 minor roads meet, particularly T junctions, are notorious accident black spots. Mini roundabouts have been installed at many such junctions, but tend to be unpopular with drivers who often feel unsure as to who has right of way, and when it is safe for them to go. Suspend your judgement for a minute: this is a deliberate part of the design! If drivers feel uncertain, they drive more carefully and less accidents result, those that do occur tending to be relatively minor (no, don't write to me about that idiot who pulled out in front of you!). Thus people have been made safer by making them feel less safe.

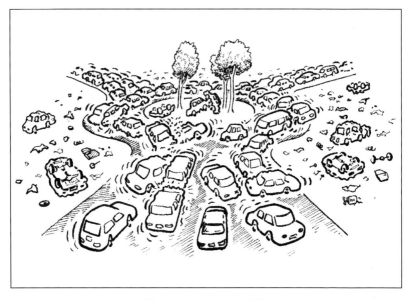

"...they drive more carefully..."

Unfortunately, the reverse is also true: the safer people feel, the worse they drive. This is one of the problems with motorways: everything seems so smooth and the fact that everyone is moving fast makes us forget how fast that is, so we tend to let the speed creep up. When something untoward occurs, the high speed leaves insufficient time to react and control the situation. I very nearly crashed my car into the back of another at the end of a motorway exit slipway, simply because I misjudged my exit speed and left braking rather late.

Psychological measures are needed to deal with this psychological phenomenon, and these have been tried via such moves as lines and bumps on the road surface being placed on the approaches to hazards. The lines start relatively wide apart, but are then drawn closer and closer together to give the mind the impression of increasing speed, with the hoped for result that drivers slow down. Many drivers would argue such methods would have no effect on their driving habits, so would be a waste of time, but experience has shown that they are beneficial and do have the desired effect. Thus another situation in which suspending judgement is desirable can be seen: where it is possible to test and experiment with solutions. No need to judge if you can 'suck it and see'.

Suspending judgement is an important element of brainstorming, a group decision making technique covered in the next chapter.

Further Examples

Some people reject the Mind Games approach because they feel that while it may work on artificial problems, it is irrelevant for real world situations. This is unwise on 2 counts; firstly, the mental suppleness and dexterity engendered by the approach are very valuable assets in all decision making, and secondly, it is factually incorrect. A vast number of instances exist where the approach has been used to successfully solve practical problems. Many of the illustrations given above were of this nature, and others are provided below.

Car Radios

Theft of car radios has been a big problem for the police, motorists and insurance companies for a number of years. While such radios can be quite expensive to replace, it is often the collateral damage done by the thief breaking the car window and ripping out wires etc. which is more expensive and troublesome. Preventing the crime directly proved extremely difficult, so the problem was reversed: prevent the thief from benefiting from the crime.

An early move was to have car radios with removable fronts or sections that the owner could take with them when leaving the car. While these worked when used, experience showed that many people found it a nuisance, and many others either forgot or just didn't bother.

Other variations to the reversal approach have been introduced including using codes which have to be entered whenever power supply to the radio has been interrupted, so that stolen radios are unusable. Police forces also automatically check the radio in all stopped vehicles to spot those with the 'wrong' radio in them, then attempt to prove they are stolen, or at least give the owner a hard time. (It is a particularly strange quirk of human nature that many people worry about theft and moan about how little the police do to prevent it, then buy a TV which 'fell off the back of a lorry').

These approaches have combined to greatly reduce demand for stolen car radios, and their theft has fallen dramatically.

Petrol Shortages

In chapter 4, I mentioned the problems caused when farmers took industrial action to block supplies. Motorists topped up their tanks at every opportunity, queues formed at garages, blocking the roads and fuelling(!) fear of supplies running out. On average, fuel tanks were almost full instead of the normal just over half full, causing increased demand at the same time as supplies were down.

Some states in the US have tried a new approach. When there is a shortage, motorists are forced to buy **at least** a certain **minimum** amount of petrol when filling up. At first sight this seems ridiculous, but on suspending judgement and thinking about it the logic becomes clear. Drivers can only buy the minimum amount once they have allowed their tank to become relatively empty. No more garage-hopping; queues disappear; demand reduces.

Children in RTAs

Thousands of children are injured in road traffic accidents each year, and the tendency has always been to blame either the child or driver for carelessness. Now it is thought that the main cause is often that the children are too small to see, or be seen by, drivers coming along a road where cars are parked.

Having challenged the assumption, and discovered a 'new', possibly common cause, attention can be focused on dealing with it. This could include bigger no parking zones near schools, more pedestrian crossings, improved driver and child training with emphasis on spotting the danger, having adults accompany children, raising the pavement outside schools, or getting children to carry placards or helium filled balloons so they can be seen above the parked vehicles.

Treating Trauma

Traditionally, if a person has been badly injured in an accident and has lost a lot of blood, the assumption has always been that they should be kept warm and given blood transfusions or other fluids to replace the lost blood and boost blood pressure. Recent thinking and experience is challenging this.

Analysis of results of traditional treatment has shown that it is very often disastrous. Boosting blood pressure often prevents blood clotting around the wound, forcing continued blood loss. In the case of brain damage, the increased flow of blood actually causes / allows the brain to suffer more damage by allowing more blood to press against the brain, and natural defence mechanisms to over-react and start 'killing' damaged areas.

Examination of the way the body naturally deals with such events has shown that, following the initial burst of adrenaline and other 'fight or flight' reactions, the body cools down, blood pressure falls, and blood drains from the extremities. Cases of 'miraculous' survival have been found e.g. where people have survived and fully recovered from being immersed ('drowned') in very cold water for up to half an hour, or during the Falklands war when some extremely badly wounded soldiers were not touched for several hours (due to either being alone or inaccessible when injured).

Many specialists are now advocating a completely new approach to major trauma cases: damage control / minimisation, allowing the body to heal itself, rather than active treatment. The body is cooled, the minimum done to control bleeding etc., and blood transfusions kept to an absolute minimum, certainly not used to re-establish 'normal' blood pressure. In the case of brain damage, the patient is cooled to a very low temperature and the brain deliberately kept virtually starved of oxygen. After a day or so, the patient is slowly brought up to normal temperature and blood supply re-established, while reactions are carefully monitored.

What is 'A Bed'

Most people would define a bed as 'somewhere to sleep', and if pushed might continue with such elements as a platform supported by four legs. The NHS definition of a bed takes up a full A4 page, and includes the little known fact that it has wheels!

This illustrates the fact that when we define something, we have to be aware of the circumstances: in the NHS, it is important that beds have wheels since they are frequently moved with patients in them.

Dating of Egyptian Dynasties

A recent television programme was concerned with the dates and order of Egyptian rulers, and how they related to those mentioned in The Bible.

The presenter had discovered that two temples, which all parties agreed had been built by two particular kings, had been built in the 'wrong' order, according to the accepted dates. He was able to prove this since the temples were built close to each other, apart from in one corner where they actually overlapped, and one of the walls of the supposedly earlier one had been built after, and cut into, one of the walls of the supposed later one.

Having discovered this, the presenter studied the justification for the original dating, and discovered that it was in part based on the name of an ancient city contained in a particular hieroglyphic. He claimed that this name had been misread by the original translator and actually referred to a different city, which had not been established until several centuries later.

Despite both these errors being pointed out, the original dates had become accepted by most researchers, and there was great reluctance to accept that they were wrong. Instead, they looked for a possible weakness in the new dates argument.

In order for the dates suggested by the presenter to be valid, there would have had to have been two rulers at the same time for a period of about 100 years. This possibility was rejected out of hand by most researchers, enabling them to discount the suggested revised dates. It could have occurred, however, if the kingdom had been split due to e.g. internal conflict.

Thus a dating system, proved on two counts to be based on incorrect information, is being clung to.

American Elections

In the presidential election between George W Bush and Al Gore, there was a complete farce with regard to the Florida votes. At least one polling station did not open, and many voters were hassled on their way to vote, but the aspect which gained most attention was the fact that the voting form itself had been designed with a confusing layout. Many people who had wanted to vote for Al Gore claimed they were unable to decide which box they should punch their hole in, so ended up not voting, while others attempted to change their mind and voted twice, or only lightly pressed the stamp over a hole, leaving only a partial punch mark on their voting paper.

Assuming it was a coincidence that George W Bush's brother was Governor of Florida, the form had presumably been designed without due attention to whether a voter would be able to understand where to put their mark. Or, perhaps an assumption had been challenged: you need most voters to vote for you if you want to win an election!

It was interesting to see how the US courts dealt with the issue. The federal courts did not want to interfere in a state matter, but also wanted justice to prevail. There was immense confusion over the legal position, including whether a full or partial recount should take place, and exactly what markings should count as votes. In the end, time took precedence over democracy, with the decision that a proper recount would take too long and possibly delay formal election of the new president beyond the traditional date. Amazing!

Rugby Backs

Everybody knew that rugby backs should be fast and relatively small so they could dodge tackles and score tries.

Along came Jona Lomu, incredibly tall and broad, but also fast and strong. Instead of dodging tackles, he brushed them off, and literally knocked over the opposing team's defences on his way to scoring plenty of tries.

Phone Books

Since phone books were first introduced, people have accepted without thought the need to look through page after page of the same last name. Then someone realised that the last name (surname) only need appear once (or, at most, at the top of each page) thereby enabling the listings to be greatly condensed, saving time and money.

Enabling Authorities

Local Authorities were set up to provide services for those in need. They became very complicated organisations, building, maintaining and running schools, leisure centres and elderly people's homes, carrying out functions such as street cleansing and refuse collection, and providing such services as fire and police.

Someone had a brain wave, and challenged the assumption that 'Local Authorities were set up to provide services'! They do not necessarily have to provide the services themselves, just ensure those people in need are able to obtain them - hence the term enabling authorities.

Adoption of this approach greatly increases the options open to the authority in that it can:
- continue to provide the service itself;
- use private contractors;
- subsidise other providers of the service, so they can provide it at a low price to the consumer;
- subsidise users of the service so they can afford to buy it from the private sector, etc.

This allows the authority to become far less complex, concentrate on the user side of the service, and be far more flexible as to how it meets the needs of its populace.

Just In Time

Manufacturers traditionally kept high stock levels of raw materials, work in progress and finished goods to help them cope with fluctuations in demand, poor quality supplies, late deliveries, breakdowns etc. These stock levels became accepted norms, but are now being challenged by some manufacturers who claim advances in quality, reliability, information technology etc. mean stocks can be greatly reduced, or ideally completely eliminated. Raw materials can instead be received and delivered straight to the production facility 'just in time' for their use. Major savings in stock holding, handling and obsolescence result, with accompanying cost reduction. Greater flexibility also enables the manufacturers to meet customer's specific requirements.

Creative Accounting

Tax evasion (deliberately falsifying records, receiving payment for goods / services in cash and not recording the transaction etc.) is illegal, but tax avoidance (taking advantage of loop holes in the law, timing acquisitions and disposals of assets so as to maximise tax relief etc.) is legal. Most taxpayers view the latter as a legitimate activity, in that it is up to the Government to draft legislation without loop holes. (Many other forms of creative accounting exist, used for particular circumstances such as to increase share prices or make raising loans easier, all aimed at placing a more favourable view on the organisation's figures than is really justified).

I accept that it would be extremely difficult to set up a system in which it would not be possible for those 'in the know' to take advantage. The problem here is that armies of tax experts exist, those working for Companies searching out new loop holes, while those working for the Government search for ways to fill the existing ones. The more imaginative and creative the individual, the more likely they are to find a new loop hole, or a way to block one. Thus many of our best brains and financial experts are spending their time counteracting and cancelling out each other's efforts with no net gain to society. If the same effort were channelled into finding a cure for baldness (quick, I'm desperate) or cancer...

Holistic Approach

There is a great tendency for solutions to be sought for specific problems, when a more holistic approach would have enabled a much more widely applicable solution to be found.

Much attention was given to carbon dioxide emissions from vehicles, and the government changed the tax to favour diesel engines. Subsequently it was discovered that the emissions from diesel engines are at least as bad as those from petrol ones. A better approach would be to assume that all vehicle emissions are dangerous until proven otherwise.

Similarly, it has been shown that lung disease is caused by asbestos fibres, coal dust and smoking. Surely it would be fair to assume all small particles are harmful until proved otherwise.

Having considered logical and mind games approaches to decision making, chapter 6 deals with group decision making, with chapter 7 completing the book by providing and demonstrating the use of a combined approach.

Self Test Questions

5.1 State 3 disadvantages of the logical approach to decision making.

5.2 What are "behavioural aspects of decision making"?

5.3 Is anticipation a wise idea when making decisions?

5.4 List 6 types of bias. Grade yourself from 0 (no bias) to 10 (extremely biased) on each type. Do you think your grading is accurate, or are you biased?

5.5 Do you agree that biases are normally "bad"? If so, how will you reduce your scores in 5.4 above?

5.6 Can mental stamina, strength and suppleness be developed through MIND BUILDING?

5.7 What 9 dots puzzle solutions did you produce? Do you accept all the others (assuming you didn't have them all) as valid?

5.8 Can you think of any personal examples where a Mind Games approach has really worked? Let me know of any great examples - I am always on the look out for them.

Exercises

5.1 List 6 factors which should influence the proportion of time spent planning as opposed to doing.

5.2 Prepare a 6x6 grid on a sheet of paper, and place the letters a-e randomly in each square. Choose a value for each letter and calculate the row and column totals. Show the results, minus one of the totals, to some colleagues and see what approaches they use to determine the missing total. After a suitable time has elapsed (say, 3 weeks!) put those using a formula approach out of their misery, and tell them to buy this book.

5.3 A friend of mine was born in March, yet her birthday is in September. Explain.

5.4 Eevil Weevil has you at his mercy: "You are going to die, but I will let you choose how" What is your reply?

5.5 Revisit exercises 2.1 and 2.2. Can you think of any Mind Games approaches that might apply?

5.6 If 16 can be expressed as 10000
and 23 as 10111
what is the expression for 27?
and what number would be represented by 1010?

5.7 a) 4 + 3 = 11   b) 10 - 5 = 4
           2 + 2 = 4   6 + 2 = 8
           5 + 5 = ?   16 - 8 = ?

5.8 A woman is heading for the middle of a field, and knows that when she gets there she will die. What makes her so sure?

5.9 "I've got 3 matchboxes, each contains 2 marbles and has a label on that should describe the marbles inside:
  2 white marbles
  2 black marbles
  1 white / 1 black

Trouble is that the labels have been mixed up and are all on the wrong boxes. If I let you look at 1 marble from 1 matchbox, could you tell me which marbles are in which matchbox?"

5.10 3 girls were sitting in a triangle facing each other. A fourth placed a hat on each of their heads, saying "I had 3 red hats and 2 blue ones. The first of you to work out the colour of the hat on her head marries the Prince or gains some other highly sexist prize. After 30 seconds, Jill won. What colour hat did she have on, and how did she work it out. (Jill didn't cheat, so nor should you!)

5.11 If you were offered a Roman coin in good condition, with a face value of 50 Dinari dated 56BC, how much do you think it would be worth in £s?

5.12 Cryptic crossword clues:
    A: River with high cards runs fast (5)
    B: Shoving sheep with some paper run riot (7)
    C: Organ beside water kops city (9)
    D: Pot I see sounds like worry (5)
    E: Carry lip shell for shell (9)

5.13 What is the phrase or saying represented by
  F: Angkooler(4,4,2,5)
  G: Revo(10)
  H: -> W son (2,4,5,3)
  I: Ground
      Railway (11,7)
  J: song song song song 8 (9)
  K: cup slip slip slip slip lip(4,1,4,5,3,3,3)

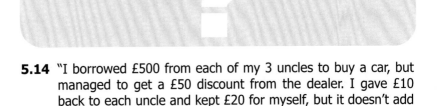

5.14 "I borrowed £500 from each of my 3 uncles to buy a car, but managed to get a £50 discount from the dealer. I gave £10 back to each uncle and kept £20 for myself, but it doesn't add up:

each uncle £490 x 3	£1470
I've got	£20
I started with	£1500

You're good with figures. Help!"

Answers to Exercises

5.1 Time available; consequences of error; degree of predictability; cost of delay; previous experience; complexity of problem.

5.3 She was born in a town called March

5.4 "Of old age"

5.5 **M25**
Ignore the problem. The more we improve travel facilities, the more people travel, so we might as well let them queue until they get so fed up that they find other routes or stop travelling.

It is tempting to say that, if my predictions of the results of global warming are correct, the weather will improve anyway! In fact, many forecasters claim that global warming may lead to a general worsening of London's weather, particularly with regard to the level of rainfall, and the frequency and severity of major storms.

Some steps have been taken to deal with the race between / to join traffic jams, for example, variable speed limits have been introduced around the M4 / M40 junction sections. When traffic volume increases, the speed limit is reduced from 70 to 60. People reach the junctions slower, so they don't get blocked, and a reduced speed limit results in faster average speed. As stated previously, it has always been difficult to get drivers to keep to any speed limit, particularly in a situation like this where one driver is likely to speed up, causing many others to react in a similar vein. It does, however, seem that these restrictions are generally obeyed, and are beneficial.

Whether this is because they are being properly enforced or that the drivers have accepted their necessity, I do not know, but the potential for widening their use to other bottleneck areas is clear. The term Gridlock was coined to refer to the situation where road junctions become blocked by each individual acting in a selfish manner. I was recently in a queue at some traffic lights where 4 vehicles in each direction had pulled forward to turn right, thereby completely blocking each other's exits.

Close some entrances and exits! at peak times to prevent people wishing to use them from cluttering up the motorway. This challenges the assumption that lots of exits reduces traffic on the motorway.

Global Warming
Search for a replacement for the Ozone layer. Could we place an artificial shield over the key areas e.g. polar caps?

Much of the problem results from too many people, so perhaps we could take massive steps to reduce population: encourage wars; tax allowances for childless couples; VAT only on food and clothing; compulsory sterilisation after 1 child; reduce health care. (Note that this goes directly against current Western thinking that we need to encourage more babies, so as to generate future labour to serve the increasing elderly population. It is, however, much more in line with, say, China, where very strict limits are being enforced regarding number of children people are allowed).

Our style of living causes problems: encourage self - sufficiency; develop information technology to discourage travel; stop all road building and maintenance.

None of the above really seem likely and I have already said that I think the Earth is doomed as far as humanity is concerned, so unless you have any ideas, perhaps we ought to start planning our exit. Will science fiction come true, with a few space craft setting off to look for a new world?

As mentioned in chapter 2, act as a selfish individual and, accepting that global warming is unavoidable, treat the symptoms and / or exploit the situation. Plan for a warmer world: look for areas currently too cold to live in which will become pleasantly warm; buy shares in sun cream manufacturers.

5.6 If 16 can be expressed as 10000
and 23 as 10111
what is the expression for 27?
and what would be represented by 1010?

The numbers are being written using a base of 2, so a 1 in the right hand column has a value of 1, a 1 in the second right column has value 2, in the third right column, value 4 and so on:

Number of column (counting from right)	Value in "normal" base 10 figures
1	1
2	2
3	4
4	8
5	16
6	32
n	2^{n-1}

16 was expressed as a 1 in the 5th column,
23 was: a 1 in the 5th column: value 16
a 1 in the 3rd column: value 4
a 1 in the 2nd column: value 2
a 1 in the 1st column: value 1

Total value: 23

27 is 16 + 8 + 2 + 1 so would be written 11011, the 0 being because there are no 4s required.

1010 would represent   1 in column 4: 8
                       1 in column 2: 2

                       Total value: 10

You may well be thinking "so what?" if you were not so polite, but in fact this "base 2" concept is vital in the world of computers. A light can be either on or off, and there can either be an electric current or not. This can be used so that a 0 is when there is no current, a 1 is when there is a current. Computers operate using series of 1s and 0s to represent numbers, letters, characters, commands etc. so the concept of "base 2" is priceless.

5.7 a)   4 + 3 = 11   b)   10 - 5 = 4
              2 + 2 = 4   6 + 2 = 8
              5 + 5 = ?   16 - 8 = ?

These questions again use the arithmetical concept of bases. We are used to counting in tens, or to base 10, which means that the number above nine is written 10 as it is 1x10 + 0.

Part a) uses 6 as the base, so that 4 + 3 gives 1x6 + 1 which is written 11.
          5 + 5 is   1x6 + 4 so it is written   14.

Part b) uses base 9, so that 10 is 1x9 + 0 = 9.
                             16 is 1x9 + 6, i.e. '15' in base 10.
                             Taking 8 from '9+6' leaves 7.
If you have trouble following the concept of different bases, ask a 7-year-old - they do this kind of thing in modern maths!

5.8   Her parachute has not opened.

5.9 If you are allowed to choose, look in the matchbox labelled 1 White / 1 Black.

Whatever colour appears (say Black) you know that box contains 2 marbles of that colour (Black) because it can't have 1 of each - the label is wrong.

The box labelled 2 of the other colour (2 White) must contain 1 White and 1 Black - it can't have 2 Black since you have found them, and it can't have 2 White if the label is wrong.

Thus the box labelled 2 of the colour you saw (2 Black) must contain the missing combination (2 White).

If forced to choose one of the other matchboxes (say 2 White) pray that a marble of that colour appears (White). The box would then have to contain 1 White / 1 Black, the other box labelled 2 of one colour (2 Black) must now contain 2 of the colour you selected (2 White) leaving the 2 of the other colour (2 Black) in the box labelled 1 White / 1 Black.

If, in that circumstance, a marble of the other colour appears (Black) you have no way of telling whether the box contains 2 of that colour (2 Black) or one of each colour. You will easily be able to get your revenge, however, by posing the next problem which is rather tricky.

5.10 Jill thought:
If any of us could see 2 blue hats, they would immediately know they had a red hat on themselves.

If any of us could see 1 blue hat, that person would know she hadn't also got a blue one on herself - because then the third one could see 2 blue hats.

Therefore we must all have red hats on. Where's that Prince?

5.11 I haven't any idea as to whether there ever was a 50 Dinari coin - or even whether Dinari was the Roman currency. What would interest me is how the person stamping the coin in 56BC would have known it was 56BC! One would have to be a little suspicious that it was a fake. If, on the other hand, it could be proved to be genuine, you would be the possessor of a coin produced by someone who knew of the exact timing of the coming of Christ 56 years before the event. Now that would be worth having.

5.12

A: River with high cards runs fast (5)
Answer: Races
Logic: R (river) + ACES (high cards) = RACES (runs fast)

B: Shoving sheep with some newspaper run riot (7)
Answer: Rampage
Logic: RAM (shove, and a sheep) + PAGE (some paper) = RAMPAGE (run riot)

C: Organ beside water kops city
Answer: Liverpool
Logic: LIVER (an organ) + POOL (water) = LIVERPOOL (city famous for the Kop)

D: Pot I see sounds like worry
Answer: Panic
Logic: PAN (pot) + I + C (sounds like see) = PANIC

E: Carry lip shell for shell (9)
Answer: Cartridge
Logic: CART (carry) + RIDGE (lip) = CARTRIDGE (outer shell of a bullet or shell)

The last was an example of the clue setter deliberately using words with many possible meanings to trick / trap / mislead the solver. I do not give any complete crosswords in this book, but they are readily available in most newspapers and in book form.

5.13

F:	Angkooler (4,4,2,5)	
Answer:	Look back in anger	
G:	Revo (10)	
Answer:	Overturned	
H:	-> W son (2,4,5,3)	
Answer:	Go west young man	
I:	Ground Railway (11,7)	
Answer:	Underground railway	
J:	Song song song song 8 (9)	
Answer:	Fortunate	
K:	Cup slip slip slip slip lip (4,1,4,5,3,3,3)	
Answer:	Many a slip twixt cup and lip	

A version of this game is available under the trade name Dingbats.

5.14 There is no reason why the net amount your uncles gave you plus the amount you have left should equal the original amount they gave you.

The original	£1500 has gone:
Car	£1450
Uncles	£30
You	£20

Chapter 6
Groups

Zulu Warrior: "One day I killed an elephant with my club!"

Tourist: "Wow, fantastic. How big is your club?"

Zulu Warrior: "There are 200 of us!"

This highlights the fact that working in groups has many potential advantages, and this applies to decision making. Other people may know some relevant information or have some good ideas, but the psychological side is of equal importance. If we expect people to carry out the decisions we make, they will be more committed to do so if they were involved in making the decision.

Assuming other people are involved in either making or implementing a decision, or are affected by it, we must be aware of the inter-relationship problems likely to arise, and the fact that they will have their own objectives which will not necessarily coincide with ours.

When making decisions in groups, considerable resources (including time, effort and money) may be required, and only justified if the quality of the decision is improved to a commensurate extent. Costs can be minimised by such measures as:
- ensuring all meetings have agendas and schedules;
- providing group members with any required reading matter well in advance;
- keeping rigidly to the agenda;
- placing time limits on individual contributions;
- avoiding excessive socialising.

Cost minimisation is not always a good thing (being an accountant, I really had to force myself to write that, and now I feel a bit dizzy and my hands are shaking). Very often there are trade-offs between time (= money), effort, and human relations. If we are too keen on keeping time and costs down, we risk putting too little effort into solving a particular problem, and consequently making a poor decision, or paying too little attention to the social and psychological needs of those involved, with possible adverse effects as outlined above. Some of the listed measures might also stifle mind management approaches such as flexible thinking.

When attempting to measure whether the quality of our decision has improved, all the benefits of group decision making should be included, as outlined above, and discussed in greater detail throughout this chapter

Two Heads are Better than One

Chapter 5 highlighted the problems that can result from rigid / inflexible problem solving, and mentioned the possibility of involving other people to counteract any biases and skill / knowledge gaps we may have as individuals.

This can be used within organisations as part of the general approach to problem solving, and on internal and external training and development courses. A major spin-off benefit of using it within an organisation is that it helps develop group behaviour, team spirit and information networks. Some commonly used methods for encouraging team work are now considered.

Master of Business Administration (MBA)

MBA philosophy is to involve people from various disciplines (marketing, production, finance, personnel) in consideration of business problems. It stems from a belief that many managers are over specialised in that they have great expertise in one field matched by great ignorance in most others! Not only do they lack knowledge in these other fields, but they also tend to have one-track minds, so that they think only in terms of their own area of expertise and the effect that any decisions they make will have in that area. The number of people undertaking MBAs, and organisations seeking to employ those with the qualification, indicates how popular this belief is.

My own roots are in accountancy, so when faced with a decision as to whether 6 new product lines should be introduced, I tended to look at the monetary effects, and particularly at profit. When I commenced studying for my MBA, it was a major shock to me that people with other backgrounds gave scant attention to money, concentrating instead on who would buy the new lines, would existing sales be affected, what pack sizes should be used, technology of production, availability of skilled personnel....

My initial reaction was to try to show them why they should be paying more attention to profit; they each tried to show the rest of us why their approach / problems were the vital ones! Pretty quickly we all realised how blinkered we had been in the past, and that understanding and consideration of all aspects of the decision was required. This is closely related to the 'challenge assumptions' idea of mind games - involving others with varied skills, knowledge and backgrounds helps us recognise some of the subconscious, often invalid, assumptions we tend to make and base decisions on.

Master of Business Administration is something of a misnomer in that the qualification is aimed at managers, not administrators. I find it interesting and highly amusing that the qualification so keenly sought by many senior managers includes such an old fashioned, misleading and almost derogatory term in its title. Administration surely implies carrying out other people's ideas and plans, rather than possession of dynamism and proactive decision making skills. Having said that, I am a great believer in the ideals underpinning the MBA approach. What's in a name?

While on my soap box, you may have noticed that I used the term personnel and not the more fashionable human resources. I hate the term human resources, being unable to view it in the intended positive light, that people are an organisation's most valuable resource and should be properly valued. I can't get away from the implication that people are just a resource like materials and equipment, there to be used and exploited to achieve the organisation's objectives.

Action-centred Learning

This is a method of confronting individuals or groups with challenges they would not normally face in their work environment. It has many potential benefits including mind building, developing decision making skills, group behaviour and team spirit, and establishing contacts and information networks.

Challenges require the solving of particular problems (can your group cross this river using only the 4 planks of wood, 6 oil drums and 10 miles of rope supplied) after which the participants are invited to discuss their approaches to the problems, and any improvements they can take with them to the next challenge and on into life. Experimentation can take place, for example as to whether it is useful to have one group member acting as leader, and what such a role should entail.

"Did he say one group member acting as leader, or ladder?"

A very useful idea is to have one of the group as an observer, seeing how the group tackles the problem, whether mind games concepts are used, the extent to which all members are involved and their ideas taken up, and reaction to 'success' and 'failure'. The purpose here is not to get their opinions so that they can comment on group performance, since the course facilitator should be carrying out that role. Instead, it is to make the observer realise how hard it is to monitor such aspects from within the group, and how often weaknesses in them are immediately apparent to an outsider. This can lead to discussion of such aspects as whether it should be common practice for groups to nominate one of their members as observer, and to what extent this should be part of the leader's role.

Most feedback should be immediate i.e. straight after each exercise, while events and timings are still fresh, and to enable the group to apply their learning while undertaking the next task. It should be backed-up with general discussion at the end of a series of exercises, or at stages throughout the course, aimed at reviewing overall progress and encouraging reflective learning.

The reason that the course facilitator should run the feedback sessions is that it is where much of the learning will take place, and it may not be done properly by an inexperienced participant. It should be detailed, constructive, group-focused, and aimed at learning, and each of these contains dangers.

Detailed feedback requires specific examples of what was good or bad, and how improvements could be made. This should be related to a decision making framework (ASK SIR L?) and performance against each element commented on. If the tasks are well designed, they will be interesting and challenging, so groups are likely to be keen to start the next one. Balance must be achieved between allowing this enthusiasm to curtail the feedback excessively, and allowing excessive feedback to frustrate, and turn the enthusiasm into general antagonism.

Constructive requires an emphasis on building on good points, not criticising bad ones: people are very often highly self critical, only too aware of their faults, but not their strengths, which often come as a surprise when pointed out to them. People do not like to have their weaknesses exposed and openly discussed, so their natural tendency in such a situation is to reject the criticism's validity, or blame other group members. Thus, a focus on the negative can quickly destroy group morale and create negative dynamics, thereby undermining future performance.

This does not mean that weaknesses should be ignored, however, but that they should be handled sensitively. Where comments are to be made regarding poor performance, they should be done constructively, often not actually mentioning the fault, instead concentrating on approaches that could have been used. If no suggestions can be thought of as to how the performance could have been improved, it can hardly be regarded as poor.

Group-focused relates to the importance of getting the group involved in the feedback: if they make points themselves, they are more likely to accept them, so good feedback will talk through the issues with the group, leading them to discover the lessons for themselves. It also relates to the general idea that positive points should be made as to individual's performance, while negative ones, if made at all, should be made of the whole group, thereby helping to avoid fragmentation and negative blame allocation.

Aimed at learning reflects that the real purpose of the exercises is to improve managerial skills such as problem solving, communication and leadership. Feedback should, therefore be focused on these issues, and not on whether the particular task was achieved. It can be very difficult to get people to accept that, although they did not succeed with the task their approach was good. It is even harder to convince them of the opposite, while still being constructive: "OK, you were successful, but your approach was all wrong and communication non-existent".

Discussion around the problem can often be highly beneficial. What particular managerial skills is the task aimed at, what are the crucial issues to be dealt with, and what other types of approach could be used? Show how the problem and solution have wider applications, particularly in the participant's 'normal' circumstances. Carry out 'what if' analysis to test the circumstances in which particular approaches would tend to work best.

Locating challenges in the outdoors, in a relatively hostile environment compared to that faced in every day life, helps break down such barriers as dress codes, status symbols and hierarchy, freeing participants to contribute fully. Inclusion of physical exertion and personal challenges, such as rock climbing, caving and canoeing, can also help achieve this, but all such aspects must be handled carefully since they can easily create new barriers themselves. An individual refusing to participate or losing their nerve in front of their colleagues could easily lose self-confidence and esteem within the organisation.

Properly designed courses should not rely on the physical attributes of participants, and entirely the wrong messages are sent if the physically strongest and fittest always win! Design will depend on the exact learning intended, but in many instances, the objective should be more in terms of 'all groups helping eachother complete the task safely and happily' rather than 'which team finishes fastest'. Indeed, challenges should be designed to 'punish' those who attempt to blast their way through instead of using their problem solving skills.

I often take groups to the Red Ridge Outdoor Pursuits Centre in mid Wales, where an endless supply of suitable challenges and tasks await. One of my favourites is where teams are faced with retrieving a small plastic camera film holder from a long (about seven feet, or a little over two metres), upright plastic pipe embedded in the ground. To make the task more enjoyable, the pipe has many holes in it, and is located in a field, about 30 yards from a stream.

Once the groups have been given the task, the obvious solution soon appears. Before reading on, spend some time thinking about how you would tackle the problem, assuming you were in a group of about 6-8 people.

The obvious solution is for some group members to bung up the holes with grass, mud, sheep droppings (abundant supply), fingers and whatever else they can think of. Others seek out containers (sheep feeding troughs, plastic fertiliser bags if lucky and the farmer has left some lying around, one group used their waterproof trousers!), fill them at the stream and pour the water into the pipe. How does that compare with your plan?

Putting the plan into action is where the fun starts, and it would not be much of a challenge if it was too easy! Since the top of the pipe is about seven feet / over two metres above the ground, ways must be found of getting the lip of the container above and near to the top of the pipe, and raising the rest of it even higher so that the water can flow down and into the pipe. Most of the water ends up on the participants - great fun in an icy March wind with two inches of snow on the ground. One or two of the group usually manage to fall over in the icy stream, and only about one group in five achieves extraction within the 30 minutes allowed.

Occasionally, a group includes a Little Ms Majik! She (or he! In real life LMMs come in all shapes, sizes and sexes) finds a strand of fence wire or long stick, and gets her assistant to secure a large dollop of sheep dropping (still plentiful supply) to one end. Obtaining vertical lift from Big Strong Lad, she inserts the wire / stick in the pipe (droppings end first) ensures a good bond between wire, droppings and case, and "out she pops". Task accomplished within five minutes, with no risk of getting soaked.

"And by the way, I saw you trying to build a raft to cross that river. Took you two hours and fell apart as soon as it hit water! Why didn't you just wade across? Its only two feet deep!"

"But I thought we weren't allowed to get our feet wet!"

"Well, you know what Mr. Thought thought? He thought his legs were sticking out of bed, so got out to tuck them in!"

"Shut up, Little Ms Majik!"

So much for the obviously right method! But how do I tell LMM that her communication skills and concern about group morale are somewhat lacking?

Brain Storming

This technique has been referred to earlier in the book, but is now considered in more detail. It is designed to enable generation of a large number of ideas, approaches and potential solutions to a problem. It is often used with the hope of finding new approaches and solutions to particularly difficult problems, or when change is so rapid that individuals are not likely to know all the relevant facts and circumstances which might make what they would assume to be an unworkable solution valid.

A group of, ideally about six people are given a problem and asked to come up with ways of tackling it. People often spark ideas in each other, are able to see ways round each other's problems, and help to generate enthusiasm, energy and hype. Groups from mixed backgrounds often perform best as they fill gaps in each other's knowledge, experience and abilities, as is often demonstrated in team quizzes when a team of super brains lacking a teenager does abysmally in rounds involving TV soaps or pop music.

Given the particular desire to find new approaches and solutions, individuals are encouraged to use their imagination, adopt or adapt each other's thoughts, suspend judgement and criticism, and generally be uninhibited. Key to success is the establishment of an atmosphere in which people are willing to throw in ideas without attempting to, even subconsciously, evaluate whether they are totally stupid, ridiculous, or have some inherent weakness that makes them completely unworkable.

Ideas are written up on white boards or flip charts so that everyone can see them, and possible connections between them established. As part of establishing and maintaining the right atmosphere, it is important that those recording the ideas do so without filtering out any they do not think are valid e.g. by only recording those ideas they like, or using negative body language or sounds to discourage thought in that area.

At the end of the session, a check should be made to ensure all ideas have been correctly recorded ready for subsequent analysis. It is important that these two steps (generation and analysis) are not merged. If the same people are involved in both stages, the second should ideally take place at least an hour after the first, since it is very difficult to suddenly change mood from one of non-critical, high energy idea generation to one of cool calm analysis and selection / rejection. If done immediately, people are also likely to be still emotionally attached to their own ideas, and unable to consider them rationally and independently. If different people are used for the second stage, it can clearly take place immediately.

As usual, there are advantages and disadvantages to both approaches. Using the same people risks emotional attachment, while fresh people may not be aware of the thought processes behind some of the suggestions.

It is possible to use the concept of brainstorming on an individual basis by listing your thoughts on paper, letting your mind run riot and adopting the other aspects of the approach. This is clearly no real substitute for the group version.

At the start of this section on brain storming I said 'Ideally about six people'. Having reached this stage in the book, you will hopefully realise that there is not going to be a particular group size ideal for all brain storming exercises. Just for fun, why not see if you can think of, say six factors (one for each person!) which would influence the optimum group size?

My immediate thoughts were:
- cost of having numerous people involved (I am an accountant!);
- breadth of knowledge / experience of this type of decision;
- type and complexity of decision;
- psychology of individuals involved e.g. willingness to participate freely and fully in a large group;
- ability of individuals to 'get their message across', but also listen to other people's contributions;
- ability of the writer to record points accurately without disturbing the flow of ideas (two writers could be used, but this tends to fragment the group / contributions);
- several people are required to generate 'heat' and benefit from the spin-off effect;
- too many people may lead to fragmentation, and frustration of people feeling their contributions are not being properly listened to and recorded;
- may also lead to a feeling of chaos and confusion. Not everyone can cope with several discussions taking place at once;
- these factors may cause some people to withdraw from the process;
- is that six yet?
- where's the kettle?

Involvement = Commitment

In addition to the fact that involving others in decision making may improve the quality of the decision, where other people are to be affected by the decision, particularly if they are required to implement it, attempts should be made to gain their commitment and acceptance.

If people are involved in decision making, they will become party to the decision and feel some responsibility for ensuring that it is successfully implemented. If, on the other hand, they are not involved but have the decision thrust upon them, no such responsibility will be felt, and indeed they may well be hostile to the decision, hoping that it fails so they can say or think "I knew it wouldn't work". People like to feel involved and that their views are respected, a fact which can be exploited, but is ignored at peril.

Another important point here is that the decision should be seen as feasible by those required to implement it, otherwise they are likely to give up any attempt to do so, concentrating their effort on tasks they think can be achieved. Given the right circumstances, most people will work hard to achieve what they view as a tough but realistic target, and if they do achieve it or come close to it, gain great satisfaction.

Many commentators felt that Mrs. Thatcher's greatest strength was her force of character, which enabled her to persuade people that her view was correct. Her basic philosophy seemed to be along the lines of 'If people disagree with me, either they must be shown why they are wrong, or replaced'. She seemed to delight in being the odd one out in arguments with other member states of the EU. Because she had a strong track record of success, very firm backing of 'grass roots' party members, and a reputation for not suffering fools gladly, few people stood up to her, and she became increasingly dictatorial.

The difficulty here is that when her view was not the right one, she was still able to gain its adoption. Hence, she was able to force through the Community Charge (or Poll Tax as it was 'popularly' known) despite the strongly held fears of many members of her own party that it would prove to be extremely unpopular and was fundamentally flawed in that it was not collectable!

One reason why the introduction of the Community Charge was always going to prove difficult to achieve was the fact that the Government failed to obtain the commitment of those responsible for its introduction. Many local authority finance staff (i.e. the people responsible for collecting the tax) felt that they had not been properly consulted when the decision to introduce the charge had been taken, were hostile to its introduction, and had predicted its failure because it would not be collectable. This hostility was exacerbated when the Government based financial data and local authority grants on the assumption of 100% collection, a figure which was clearly unachievable and therefore removed any possibility of success from those faced with the task of collection. Thus they had no commitment to its success, and a psychological desire for it to fail so that they would be proved right.

This duly occurred, as demonstrated by the Poll Tax riots, and fact that billions of pounds of Community Charge had to be written off due to inability of the relevant local authorities, particularly London boroughs, to collect it. They were unable to maintain sufficiently accurate occupancy details, or trace former residents once they had moved. Turnover of occupants was much higher than had been anticipated by the government. The government were forced to back down, and replaced Community Charge with Council Tax.

Ultimately, this was a major factor in Mrs. Thatcher's downfall, so her domineering personality, which had helped her achieve her greatest triumphs, eventually led to her demise: all things contain the seeds of their own destruction.

Individuals who have participated in decision making only to find their views rejected or ignored may become extremely frustrated and angry, particularly if they feel the consultation was only a sham and the decision had already been made. The House of Commons is a case in point in that the government often has such a large majority that there is no prospect of it losing an important vote. The opposition huff and puff, but they can't blow the House down, and their frustration often shows. This does not mean that the debates are a waste of time in that at least the policies and actions of the Government are openly debated and the electorate does ultimately have the final say.

Communication

Each individual within a group will tend to perceive a particular problem in their own way, which could result in the group effectively trying to solve a number of different problems instead of the one it is genuinely facing. In the extreme, the real problem can be a failure to communicate properly, such that once all the facts are known, the problem disappears, or effectively solves itself.

In order to solve a problem in, or involving, a group, good communication, both oral and written, is vital, including:

- sender's name and credentials
- intended recipients
- date and time
- contact address
- subject matter
- intended / suitable uses
- information sources
- assumptions
- information used
- reliability
- analysis and conclusions
- possible actions
- recommendations, with explanation
- required feedback

Of course, much of the above may already be known by the recipient and, therefore, **_at the sender's risk_** not included. Two Hollywood stars are reputed to have sent the following messages to each other:

Original	Reply
'Where?'	'My place'
'When?'	'Tonight'

Whether they both knew what the other had in mind is pure conjecture, but as you will recall from chapter 2 (this is one of my favourite phrases, being a polite way of effectively saying 'if you have been paying attention, you should already know this') feedback is necessary to confirm the communication was received, understood and acted upon.

I do not know whether you are enjoying this book, attempting every exercise, and learning all sorts of interesting new facts and ideas. I have my suspicions, but I don't know! In fact, you would be a biased sample even if I did know, because anyone not doing the above would presumably have stopped reading it long ago. There, you show great faith and commitment to me by reading all this, and I reward you by calling you a biased sample!

I do know I have been misled several times by messages left on my desk saying no more than "The meeting's off" or similar. Cryptic clues are good for keeping the mind flexible, but this is ridiculous!

I know that some recipients are dumb, but it is almost always the sender's fault if the message is misinterpreted. Do not assume the intended recipient will receive, understand, and act on your message: assume makes an ass out of u and me. I very nearly learnt this the hard way when, teaching my son how to use a hammer, I held a nail against a piece of wood and said "When I nod my head, you hit it". Luckily he missed! This kind of misunderstanding is often called system noise or interference, other examples being two notices I saw outside a local church:

> **DO YOU KNOW WHAT HELL IS?**
> Come and hear our new organist

> **IF YOU ARE TIRED OF SIN - COME IN**
> (the alternative being added by a local wit)
> if not, ring 01245 493131

Or, in the small ads. column of a newspaper:

FOR SALE: GREAT DANE, WILL EAT ANYTHING
very fond of children

FOR SALE: HEARSE
Body in good condition

While some graffiti I once read said:
MY MOTHER MADE ME A HOMOSEXUAL
(to which had been added)
If I get her the wool, will she make me one?

Instructions I was once given as to how to get to a particular rugby ground included "turn right at the last roundabout" which assumed I knew the last roundabout when I saw it! Similarly, a telephone message telling me to "Bake at two-twenty" left me unsure whether we were talking Fahrenheit or Celsius, when it was actually referring to twenty minutes past two!

The above illustrate the difficulties and ambiguities of language, but other problems abound. People have different backgrounds and experiences, causing different values, attitudes, beliefs, skills and knowledge. We also each have certain expectations and allow ourselves to think in terms of stereotypes, which in turn leads on to selective perception and prejudice, a topic discussed in chapter 5. All of the above result in our viewing the same events differently.

A favourite joke of mine is a cartoon depicting a man standing in snow up to his thighs, saying to his son "This is nothing. When I was your age, the snow was so deep it came up to my chin". Next to him, of course, is his young son struggling to keep his head poking out of the snow.

Hidden Agendas

When taking part in the decision making process, people often have their own secret objectives as well as the stated ones. They might be looking for an easy life, to increase their own importance in the organisation, or to get you sacked! Equally, they may have fears about a possible change such as whether they can cope, will their existing easy life be threatened, or will they have to admit to knowing nothing about the internet. If you can determine someone's hidden agenda, particularly without them realising it, it might help you argue the case in such a way as to gain their support.

" Here, little Johnnie let me pay for you to go to the pictures."

It is often possible, by adding a few sweeteners, to make a scheme attractive to someone who would have otherwise been against it. Often the final decision consists of a package, each element of which is designed to meet an individual's objectives - called "building a camel" in chapter 2 to reflect the concept that, while it may not be a racehorse, at least it gets the job done and in certain circumstances is the best solution! (If you want to know the joke about the camel and two house bricks, e-mail j.j.rayment@apu.ac.uk but do have the decency to include a joke for me. As you will know by now, it doesn't matter how old, feeble and corny it is!)

In general, we need to think about our proposal from the viewpoint of other people involved, and explain it to them in a manner they will find acceptable. Too often a confrontational approach is adopted when a win-win solution (i.e. one in which both parties are better off) could have been found. Instead of responding to a wage claim by threatening redundancy, could a productivity / quality package be agreed which would result in higher sales and more added value to be shared between the workers, managers and owners? (oops, nearly forgot: I guess the Government will want a share too!)

Often, there will not be a solution which suits all parties involved in the decision, so a compromise will have to be agreed. Experienced negotiators may be able to use this situation to their advantage by initially adopting a tough position and then appearing to generously give ground when in reality they are only moving to what was a realistic position in the first place. This kind of posturing can be very divisive and time consuming, and backfire if taken too far, with one party feeling insulted by a derisory offer and withdrawing completely from the negotiation. This can happen with wage negotiations, when the managers start by making an offer which is so low that the union side react by striking.

If the problem under consideration is particularly sensitive or there is concern over maintaining confidentiality, involving other people may be felt to be an unnecessary risk. This would be particularly likely if one of the options under consideration would be disadvantageous to those normally involved in the decision making process.

Group Behaviour

When people work in groups they develop codes and standards of behaviour which may be very different from the organisation's official ones. Provided they are not too disruptive, it is often better to allow these group norms to continue rather than attempt to force the group to conform to company rules and regulations.

It is often claimed that groups go through four developmental stages:

Forming: – initial coming together, ice breaking and setting up basic relationships;
Norming: – setting up unofficial practices and behaviours;
Storming: – challenging relationships, practices and behaviours, clearing the air to facilitate:
Performing: – achieving the task.

"Which stage do you think we are at?"

Within the group, the views and suggestions of certain individuals are likely to be given greater credence than those of others. This will often at least partially reflect any official structure or hierarchy which exists, but many other forms of power and influence will have an effect:

Physical: - Physical strength is far less advantageous in a modern group setting than it used to be. It is also officially viewed negatively if people are felt to be attempting to exploit their sexuality to obtain their objectives. It is interesting to note, however, how many advertisements are based on these - often being of handsome, 'fit' men, presumably aimed at women. As stated in chapter 4, psychologists have also discovered that tall people are more successful in interviews;

Knowledge: - Both general and specific, a particular variation of this being the possession of qualifications. I have known people to be treated completely differently immediately on qualifying, suddenly gaining stature and credibility, and their decisions being accepted without question;

Experience: - Particularly if known to have been successful when faced with a similar task in the past;

Charisma: - An attractive personality;

Oratory: - Ability to persuade others;

Managerial: - Ability to handle decision making etc.;

Crisis: - Known not to panic, but instead come up with practical, workable, solutions.

What is important here is the group's perception of the individual, not that person's true abilities. A shy person may possess a vast amount of experience and knowledge, but not have much influence on the group's behaviour and decision making due to failure to communicate effectively with other group members. It is also sometimes possible for an individual to obtain temporary high influence by falsely claiming relevant experience or knowledge, the question being whether they are found out before they move on. One of the most important roles of a chairman is to ensure each group member's opinions are given due weight.

Another kind of power is **negative** power, the ability to disrupt the smooth operation of the organisation's affairs. An individual's negative power can be out of all proportion to their position in the hierarchy, thus the Managing Director's secretary may only be a 'scale 3', but able to prevent you gaining access to a highly influential person, and a junior computer operator could "accidentally" wipe some vital information or spill a cup of coffee while sitting at the keyboard. Unions have become very effective at using negative power by only calling key personnel out on strike.

Organisations sacking individuals with high negative power often do so in what may seem at first sight an extremely harsh manner e.g. sudden announcement, followed by immediately escorting them off the premises, having their personal belongings brought out to them. The reason for such an approach is the fear that the individual will make use of their negative power to seriously disrupt the organisations functions: "wipe the hard disk" or something equally evil.

"If it's so clever, let's see if it can fly!"

A particular concern when looking at group decision making is the fact that groups sometimes make extremely poor decisions, which some of the individuals involved should definitely have known were wrong. Reasons for this type of behaviour, dubbed Groupthink by Janis, include:

- lack of individual responsibility;
- unwillingness to break group norms or appear disloyal;
- placing consequences on themselves above the overall consequences of the decision (e.g. fear of being disciplined for 'breaking ranks');
- automatically following a standard approach (one of the main weaknesses in systematic decision making covered in chapter 4).

This scenario tends to occur with most dramatic effect when a group is faced with a slowly worsening situation. Possibly acting like a panfull of frogs in slowly boiling water, no-one wants to be the first to jump! An extremely well known example was the Battle of the Somme, with individual officers perfectly aware that continual assaults on enemy lines were basically futile and extremely costly in terms of casualties, but not prepared to force through a change of tactic.

Any long-standing group could suffer from this phenomenon, with the House of Commons a very clear example: everyone knows their rules, regulations and processes are terribly out of date, with promises being made as to improved provision of facilities for female MPs, and much earlier start and finish times for Parliament sessions, but little progress is made.

A recent television programme investigated the USA's Apollo mission which exploded shortly after take-off. It claimed that, despite strong warnings from the engineers involved in the project that the craft was not safe, the NASA committee responsible for the launch decided to go ahead. Several individuals on the committee were interviewed and admitted that they had extreme misgivings about the launch, one even stating that he had gone home to his wife and told her that disaster was inevitable. None had been prepared to be the one to call a halt.

'The King's New Clothes' is a well-known tale, and an excellent illustration of this kind of situation / behaviour. Everyone knew that the King was naked, but no-one was prepared to say so. Of course, there may have been any number of reasons why they kept quiet - some people might enjoy the sight of the King revealed in all his glory and looking somewhat foolish. As with most tales of this nature, it can be read in many different ways and at different levels. Another interpretation is to do with 'power': very often people in powerful positions try to push through their desires based on false / invalid arguments - in other words, they have 'no clothes'. This interpretation fits extremely well with the Groupthink one because an underlying cause of Groupthink is often the reluctance of subordinates to openly contradict the viewpoint of their superiors even if they know them to be wrong.

The end of the story is also a very good illustration of how the problem can often be dealt with. A young boy, blissfully unaware of the niceties of the situation, stated what everyone knew: the King has got no clothes! Insiders who attempt to play this role often attempt to justify their actions by use of such phrases as 'playing devil's advocate', but the very fact that they feel the need to do so highlights the quandary they are faced with. For this reason, it can be very useful to have an 'ignorant' and independent outsider involved in group decision making, tasked with stating what others can't. (It is also often beneficial, when making decisions alone, to get someone to play such a role).

In the middle ages, when I was a lad, the monarch was surrounded by her / his court, and one of the important members was the Court Jester, or Fool, whose main function was to carry out the role under discussion. Given the instability of court life, and the constant fear of rebellion or treason, it would have been very dangerous for a high ranking and powerful individual to criticise the monarch's plans, but someone had to do it. Hence, the idea of a Fool, who could speak the unspeakable, be openly mocked, but on occasion ensure that important aspects were in fact considered. Shakespeare's King Lear is taught the error of his ways by his Fool.

Team Balance

Individuals often have a particular role within a team which they perform well. This can be anything from generating good ideas, getting tasks completed, or simply keeping the team harmonious. Attempts should be made to ensure groups are well balanced and members are allowed to adopt their natural role. Too many 'ideas people' in a team could mean that it never actually finishes tasks assigned to it - members either continually come up with new approaches, or just become bored and move on to new challenges.

Other aspects need balancing too. A mix of specialists and generalists will ensure that both aspects are covered, while having some experienced and some inexperienced people will help the inexperienced develop, and allow the group to benefit from their fresh ideas, approaches and enthusiasm. Whizz kids are likely to be hot on current developments, have broad experience and represent future top management, while plodders have a thorough knowledge of the area under consideration and are less likely to move on part way through the process. A mix of personalities (introvert / extrovert etc. as covered in chapter 5) will also be beneficial.

A well - balanced team!

The above assumes freedom to select the membership of the team, and that the desired attributes are available in the potential members. This will not be the case very often, so you should try to establish the particular strengths and weaknesses of any individuals and teams you become involved with so as to be able to make allowances for them.

This chapter considered the importance of involving others in our decision making, and the related behavioural aspects. Chapter 7 pulls together the various aspects of decision making and recommends a combined approach aimed at ensuring we use the correct elements of each technique for the particular decision confronting us.

Self Test Questions

6.1 What is the MBA philosophy regarding training needs of managers?
Do you think it is valid?

6.2 Should action-centred Learning courses be voluntary or compulsory (or banned)?

6.3 Under what conditions is brainstorming likely to work best?

6.4 List 6 behavioural / psychological reasons why involving people in decisions that will affect them is a good thing.

6.5 And 6 problems with group decision making

6.6 And 10 inclusions in good communications

6.7 Is there a difference between Feedback and System Noise? Are they both good things?

6.8 What are Hidden Agendas, Group Norms and Negative Power?

6.9 Do you have a natural team role? If so, what? (it better not be centre half!)

6.10 List 6 factors to consider when trying to produce a balanced team.

Exercises

6.1 Spend 5 minutes listing points to be considered if buying a new house. If possible, get a group of colleagues to do the same thing as a brainstorming exercise. Compare the lists with each other and the one given in the answers section below. What differences can you see, and can you explain them?

6.2 Think about some group decisions that you have been involved with, and complete the following for each:

- Description of Problem
- Size of Group
- Your Role
- Other Peoples' Roles
- Length of Meetings
- Number of Meetings
- Group Organisation
- Decisions Made
- Level of Agreement
- Implementation Plans
- Any other Aspects

What were your feelings at the time regarding:
- Likelihood of Successful Implementation
- Frustration / Elation etc.
- Other Team Members
- Value for Money (i.e. was the time / cost / effort put into the decisions well spent?)

Did these feelings prove justified?

Having completed this exercise, consider the extent to which your comments reflect those made in the chapter about the behavioural aspects of decision making.

Answers to Exercises

6.1 Brainstorming Exercise: Points to consider when buying a new house

- cost
- location: proximity to schools / buses / trains / airports / motorways / shops / work (not too near, not too far) / other amenities / good areas for running or walking
- noise
- other environmental aspects e.g. factories / too near a popular pub / local traffic density
- age; state of repair; central heating / double glazing
- size: overall / no. of rooms + their sizes; types of rooms; potential for expansion
- view; could surroundings be altered e.g. by new building
- neighbours
- garage and parking
- garden size / design / condition
- TV reception - which channels / quality
- distance from current house / friends / relatives
- reputation of area / quality of surrounding houses

This list was prepared by me in a solo 5 minute brainstorming exercise. Contents are fairly jumbled and random, with some factors of major importance and others possibly irrelevant!

Comparing my list with yours, or any other individual's would be expected to reveal gaps in each. These could be partially filled by simply combining the lists, but if the theory of group brainstorming is valid, one would expect a group version to be superior to even this combined list, due to the spin-off effects.

If the group list was not superior, it could be because the session was badly managed. As stated in this chapter, running brainstorming sessions effectively is a skill which requires practice.

As covered in chapters 2 and 3, the next problem would be to decide how important different factors are, possibly by ranking and weighting them. It would then be possible to score available houses on each factor, apply the weighting, and come up with a ranking of their relative overall desirability.

In practice, this is not as easy as it sounds since there may be several people's views to take into consideration and each will weight and score factors and individual houses differently. Garden size would be interesting here: one might automatically think 'the bigger the better', but some people may hate gardening or the thought of children wanting to play and possibly breaking windows or bringing mud in the house. Using a mind games approach might offer the best of both worlds: buy a house with a small garden, but close to a park.

Often the house which has the highest weighted score will just not feel right, or another which scores relatively badly will have some hidden attraction. If this is so, it actually reflects the fact that the weightings and scores are not fully valid, so reality should prevail. This does not mean the process has been a waste of time: it has achieved its objective of helping you make a decision!

Chapter 7
A Combined Approach

**With problems to solve ASK SIR L
And Ms Majik to cast you a spell
Both the girl and the knight
'Cos to solve problems right
I find Logic and Magic Group swell!**

The following elements of decision making have been covered in this book:

Logical:	Problem Solving Decision Making Risk Analysis
Magical:	Mind Games Why important Possible drawbacks
Groups:	Use in Decision Making Advantages Behavioural Aspects

This chapter brings together these elements to help you apply the relevant parts of each to whatever problems and decisions you face.

To provide a summary and guide for your future use, a checklist approach is adopted. To illustrate its practical application, the list is then used to consider the problem: How Could Hospital Waiting Lists Be Cut?

The checklist has the ASK SIR L Logical approach as a framework to ensure all relevant facets are considered, a wide range of options generated, the optimum solution selected and implemented, and any available lessons learnt.
In recognition of the inherent weaknesses in relying solely on a

systematic approach, a Magical Mind Games section has been added, containing ideas and methods to challenge conventional approaches and assumptions, and encourage use of intuition.

Consideration and involvement of others in problem solving is also important, so a section on Groups deals with the inherent problems and behavioural considerations, and approaches to dealing with them.

Mind Games and Groups need to be considered at every stage of the ASK SIR L model, but to avoid repetition I have only included each of them once. Mind Games is covered first, since it is vital to get off to the right start, and I have placed Groups after Solutions because it is in the area of Solutions and Implementation that Groups are of most importance. So, the revised model can be summarised as MASKS GIRL! I leave you to decide whether this represents Sir L trying to keep Little Ms Majik hidden, her ability to see through the issues masking the real problem, or something else entirely: possibly an indication that I am Mind Morphing on the Fine Line again!

A number of analytical and strategic management techniques complete the list, despite the fact that they have not all been covered in this book. They are included mainly as a reminder to anyone familiar with the techniques that they may be relevant. If you are not familiar with one that looks as though it could be useful for your problem, try the relevant section in your local library! If that does not work, you can always e-mail me, and for an (al)most reasonable fee....

When considering specific parts of the list, particularly if attempting to solve a genuine problem, it may be beneficial to re-read the part of the book that dealt with that section. That will help refresh your mind as to exactly what each section entails, and examples of its practical use.

As with most checklists, this one is not exhaustive. Problems come in an infinite number of guises, and it would be misleading to claim any list covered every possible consideration for them all. Such a list would, in any case, be extremely long, dry, monotonous and boring (so, what's new?) and include much which was irrelevant to any particular problem. It would result in all the worst elements of the systematic approach: artificial, formulaic, stinted, backward looking, unimaginative, and inflexible.

Instead, my objective is to give you a list that will help stimulate, rather than stifle, your thinking about a problem. You might think some of the things I have included are superfluous, or know of ideas or approaches that I have left off. The behavioural approach would claim that you would not really accept the list as 'yours' until you have customised it to your own way of thinking. Feel free to play around and make it your list - maybe give yourself a target of, say two changes to each section, or insert a whole new section of your own. Maybe do something really daring and turn it into a matrix or mind-map: make Little Ms Majik really proud of you!

Here comes the checklist. **Enjoy!**

DECISION MAKING CHECKLIST

Magical Mind Games

- **Tackle Weaknesses of Logical Approach:**
  - ⇨ Fragmentation
  - ⇨ Rigidity
  - ⇨ Invalid assumptions
  - ⇨ Outmoded methods and processes
  - ⇨ Artificial boundaries
  - ⇨ Bias and prejudice
- **Challenge Assumptions:**
  - ⇨ Problem boundaries and possible solutions
  - ⇨ Is there a quick obvious solution?
  - ⇨ Is it 'your' problem?
  - ⇨ Is it an opportunity e.g. to obtain backing or assistance with a bigger problem?
  - ⇨ Are the obvious, traditional causes the actual ones?

- **Flexible Thinking:**
  - ⇨ Look for new approaches and solutions
  - ⇨ New thought processes and patterns
  - ⇨ New analogies
  - ⇨ Wide range of solutions
  - ⇨ Target number of solutions
  - ⇨ Mental imagery

- **Mind Games Techniques:**
  - ⇨ Different angles
  - ⇨ Suspend judgement
  - ⇨ Problem reversal
  - ⇨ Dominant ideas
  - ⇨ Crucial factors
  - ⇨ Holistic approach

- **Unconventional Approaches:**
  - Do nothing
  - Deliberately delay decision and implementation
  - Involve children and outsiders
  - Role play

Logical (Part 1)

i. **Appreciate**
- **Ensure all potential problems are identified, using such techniques as:**
  - Environmental scanning
  - Competitor and market analysis
  - Internal analysis
  - SWOT analysis and strategic review
  - 'Worst case' scenario
  - Automatic early identification of problems
  - Employees look for and report potential problems

- **New activities:**
  - Possible problems
  - Inherent risks

- **Systems reviews / testing:**
  - Risk management
  - Test equipment to check functionality
  - Control, reporting, feedback

- **Comparison:**
  - 'What is happening' v 'what should be happening'
  - Standard v actual
  - Significant difference?

- **Is it 'your' problem?!**

- **Approach to adopt:**
    - Logical or magical
    - Psychological
    - Models, simulations, numerical
    - Trial and error, experimentation
    - Piecemeal or 'big bang'

ii. **Specify**
- **The problem or risk**
    - Definition
    - Is apparent problem the real one, or just a symptom?
    - Likelihood of occurrence
    - Consequences of various outcomes
    - Scope and focus
    - Objectives: Smart, specific, measurable, achievable, relevant, time-related.
    - What would constitute "success"

- **Importance:**
    - Need / ability to act
    - Effort to put into solving it
    - If ignored, will problem worsen, lessen, solve itself?
    - Is it current, real, urgent, major, long-term, work-related?
    - Or speculative, planning, minor, private, educational, for fun, a game?

- **Resources available for analysis and solutions:**
    - time, money, facilities (e.g. computer power), people with...
    - Relevant knowledge / experience / attitude

- **Exactly what Is (and is not) going wrong:**
    - Establish facts, experiment, test
    - Size, scope, duration
    - Influence of trends, cycles, seasonal factors

- ⇨ Degree of certainty
- ⇨ Accuracy of measurement
- ⇨ Who, What, Where, Why, When, How?
- ⇨ But not...
- ⇨ Weight for likelihood / importance
- ⇨ Genuine investigation: see for yourself

iii. Causes
- **Cause and effect relationships:**
    - ⇨ What might happen? - What did happen?
    - ⇨ Who, What, Where, Why, When, How?
    - ⇨ But not...
    - ⇨ What could have caused the problem? Potential, possible and actual
    - ⇨ Which cause is most likely?
    - ⇨ Weight for likelihood / importance
    - ⇨ Single or multiple causes, required chain of events
    - ⇨ Brainstorm
    - ⇨ Real, hidden, underlying causes
    - ⇨ Beware accepting a particular cause too easily
    - ⇨ Use deduction to help establish underlying logic / validity
    - ⇨ Prove the suspected cause was the actual cause

- **Common causes include:**
    - ⇨ Stupidity, carelessness, ignorance, excess speed or haste
    - ⇨ Staff quality and availability
    - ⇨ Mechanical breakdown, lack of systems or alarms, breaches of security
    - ⇨ Chain of events, weak link breaking
    - ⇨ Inability to cope with change, failure to adjust to new circumstances
    - ⇨ Poor communication, invalid assumptions
    - ⇨ Inadequate escape routes: existence, awareness, available, accessible

iv. Solutions
■ **Generation:**
- ⇨ Brainstorm
- ⇨ Team, to avoid bias / fill skill and knowledge gaps
- ⇨ Tackle causes
- ⇨ Or deal with effects and symptoms
- ⇨ Break the chain of events
- ⇨ Restrict access via 'fire walls', passwords and physical security
- ⇨ Really will solve the problem and achieve objectives
- ⇨ Lessen likelihood / consequences of a damaging event occurring
- ⇨ Avoid: don't do the activity
- ⇨ Transfer risk: contract terms / insurance
- ⇨ Carry risk
- ⇨ Protect high risk / consequence areas: equipment and staff cover
- ⇨ Take precautions: safety belts, helmets
- ⇨ Automatic action e.g. sprinklers, doors close

■ **Selection:**
- ⇨ Timing of decision: detailed planning means delayed action
- ⇨ Research, analysis, investigation, selection
- ⇨ Relevant factors, relative importance, weightings
- ⇨ Models for selection:
  * Plus and minus points
  * Key factors
  * Weighted scoring, expected value
  * Formulae, spreadsheets, 'what if' analysis
- ⇨ Phased analysis:
  * Rough analysis to identify obviously unsuitable solutions
  * Detailed appraisal of remaining

- ⇨ Phased solutions, with bail out and cut off points
- ⇨ Trials, models, simulations
- ⇨ Test in all plausible circumstances
- ⇨ Short and long term aspects: quick fix or long term solution?
- ⇨ Trade-off: risks and benefits
- ⇨ Attempt to overcome weaknesses in potential solutions
- ⇨ Solution package
- ⇨ Ability to implement
- ⇨ Realistic, politic
- ⇨ Certainty of results
- ⇨ Side effects
- ⇨ Consequences of failure or solution going wrong
- ⇨ Weight for e.g. cost, speed, certainty, quality
- ⇨ Value for money: economy, efficiency, effectiveness
- ⇨ Fair, equitable and acceptable to affected parties

Groups

■ **Group Psychology:**
- ⇨ Avoiding blame by denying the problem or possible causes
- ⇨ Ignoring or understating of risks
- ⇨ Complacency or ostrich management
- ⇨ Doom mongers
- ⇨ Groupthink: acting like lemmings
- ⇨ Media hype; over-reaction
- ⇨ Effects of rumour
- ⇨ Assuming one result proves or disproves validity of approach or decision
- ⇨ Bias
- ⇨ Falsification or manipulation of facts
- ⇨ Invalid conclusions
- ⇨ Desire for fame or glory

■ **Own Psychology:**
- ⇨ Bite the bullet! Don't put off 'nasty' or important actions
- ⇨ Need to be seen to act, take the sting out of the situation
- ⇨ Or deliberate delay: be seen not to panic or over react

■ **Establish Correct Atmosphere:**
- ⇨ Attitude to whistleblowers
- ⇨ Work within people's comfort zones
- ⇨ Fit their image
- ⇨ Avoid personal attacks and a blame culture
- ⇨ Positive attitude: "Change = Challenge = Growth"
- ⇨ Consider stage of group development: form, norm, storm, perform

■ **Force Field Analysis:**
- ⇨ Forces for and against, relative strengths, how to influence
- ⇨ Consider resistance and inertia: need to keep pushing
- ⇨ Look for inability to cope and negative attitudes, both active and passive
- ⇨ Attitude Spectrum:
  - * Champion - disciple - accept - cope - unconcerned - passively reject - actively reject
  - * How to move people towards the start of this list?
  - * One step at a time, complete conversion, or removal?
- ⇨ Sources of influence and power:
  - * Position, experience, reputation, knowledge, skill, networks, persuasion, charisma
  - * Negative power

■ **Look for Allies:**
- ⇨ Influential, popular; champions
- ⇨ Networking and deals: build a camel

■ Gain Commitment:
- ⇨ Involvement from the start
- ⇨ "Your" change becomes "our" change
- ⇨ Accepted as reasonable and achievable
- ⇨ Consult: encourage contributions and participation
- ⇨ In both planning and execution
- ⇨ Keep (and be seen to be) flexible
- ⇨ Demonstrate effectiveness:
    * other users
    * good planning

■ 'Sell' the Change:
- ⇨ Explain the need for change
- ⇨ Their problem as well as yours
- ⇨ Look for common ground, emphasise extent of agreement
- ⇨ Consider the effects on others, and their viewpoint
- ⇨ What constraints and practicalities will they be faced with?
- ⇨ Hidden agendas
- ⇨ Show how they will benefit or can minimise their losses
- ⇨ Help them do so

■ Introduce Slowly:
- ⇨ Spoon-feed: allow time to digest and absorb
- ⇨ Success is proportional to time allowed
- ⇨ Initial awareness, first formal approach, feasibility, commitment, details etc.

■ Boost Morale:
- ⇨ Frequent communication, verbal and written, particularly of success
- ⇨ Political withholding of information, or selective presentation
    * May be necessary, but is dangerous
    * People will not be pleased if they find out
    * Long term trust may be threatened

Logical (Part 2)
v. Implement
- **Project management:**
  - Plans including programme, networks, critical path and budgets
  - Key result areas, milestones, phases
  - Fall-back position, in case things go wrong
  - Cut-off and bail-out points
  - Dry runs, contingency plans
  - Feedback of results, to check all is OK

- **Piecemeal approach:**
  - 'Swiss cheese', eat an elephant
  - Pilot schemes with champions
  - Easy / certain success areas first
  - Gain credibility / acceptance / enthusiasm

- **Or 'Big Bang':**
  - Over in one go
  - Quick adoption and benefits
  - Less potential for confusion
  - Concentrated effort
  - Less chance for resistance to build

- **Have a long-term strategy:**
  - Change is costly (money and time)
  - But benefits outweigh costs
  - Tackle inertia and resource allocation drag
  - Training and courses (including psychological effect)
  - Reward successful implementation

- **Individual responsible, backed by working parties etc.:**
  - ⇨ Consultants for specialist expertise / experience
  - ⇨ Or to do the dirty work
  - ⇨ Use transformation experts if necessary
  - ⇨ But beware long-term consequences

vi. Review
- **Has the problem been solved?:**
  - ⇨ Are the objectives being achieved?
  - ⇨ Has full implementation been achieved?
  - ⇨ Are all elements of the solution working?
  - ⇨ Are outputs as expected?

- **Compare actual to plan:**
  - ⇨ Allow for any time-lags

- **Can any shortcomings be identified and their causes established?:**
  - ⇨ Do they relate to a particular part of the solution?

- **Depending on outcome:**
  - ⇨ Approve as successful
  - ⇨ Commence next phase, with adaptations if necessary
  - ⇨ Repeat whole problem solving process!

vii. Learn
- **Beware being 'wise after the event':**

- **Could problems of this nature be avoided in future?:**
  - ⇨ Scenario planning
  - ⇨ Disaster and contingency plans

- ➪ Escape routes
- **Did the decision making approach prove effective?:**
  - ➪ Could any elements of it be improved?
  - ➪ Is it too slow or expensive?
  - ➪ Is the balance right between planning and doing?
  - ➪ Invalid models: logical flaws, missing / weak rungs

- **To what extent are any shortcomings due to:**
  - ➪ The decision model
  - ➪ Incorrect use
  - ➪ Poor implementation
  - ➪ Unforeseen events
  - ➪ Or just bad luck?

- **Do we need to improve our decision making and implementation skills?:**
  - ➪ Is good use being made of mind games approaches as relevant?
  - ➪ Do we suffer from 'groupthink'?
  - ➪ Need for education, skill development, training, practice?
  - ➪ Action-centred, and wide-ranging: logical, mind games, behavioural

- **Are decisions taken in groups when appropriate?:**
  - ➪ Properly run, with a leader and observer?
  - ➪ Affected parties properly considered, involved and informed?

- **How is all this new knowledge going to be shared throughout the organisation?:**
  - ➪ Written procedures, models, and bullet point lists
  - ➪ Checks to ensure and confirm all the above has actually happened?

Analytical Techniques
- **Cost Analysis:**
  - Linear regression
  - Cost - volume - profit analysis
  - Opportunity costs, relevant costs
  - Activity - based costing

- **Investment Appraisal:**
  - Discounted cash flow, net present value
  - Probability, expected value
  - Value for money, cost-benefit analysis

- **Planning:**
  - Linear programming
  - Budgeting
  - Network and critical path analysis

- **Performance Appraisal:**
  - Variance analysis
  - Ratio analysis, benchmarking

Strategic Management Techniques
- **Analysis Of The External Environment**
  - PESTLED:
  - Political, economic, societal, technological, legal, ecological, demographic
  - 'Green' moral and ethical issues

- **Internal Analysis:**
  - Financial and operational gearing
  - Porter's value chains, added value
  - Product portfolio:
    * Product range, loss leaders, product life cycle

* Boston Matrix (market share and potential growth)

■ **Market Analysis**
- ⇨ Porter's 5 Forces (suppliers, buyers, substitute products, new entrants, and existing competitors)

■ **Strategic Options**
- ⇨ Porter's 3 generic strategies (cost leadership, differentiation, specialisation)
- ⇨ Ansoff's Matrix (new or old products, in new or old markets)
- ⇨ Market penetration or skimming
- ⇨ Marketing mix: product, place, price, promotion
- ⇨ TQM (total quality management)
- ⇨ Focus on customers
- ⇨ 'Lean' organisations and 'just in time' philosophy
- ⇨ Business process re-engineering

■ **Performance Appraisal**
- ⇨ Kaplan and Norton's Balanced Scorecard
- ⇨ Benchmarking

Having provided you with a decision-making framework and checklist, I now give the opportunity to try it out on the following problem:

How could Hospital Waiting Lists be Cut?

My thoughts are shown opposite, but you should prepare your own ideas before reading mine.

HOW COULD HOSPITAL WAITING LISTS BE CUT?

Mind Games

Why does the length of waiting lists matter? Surely, the real problem is the time before people are treated, not how long a list is. Should we redefine the problem to be "How to cut waiting time for treatment"?

This might at first sight appear to be a rhetorical question: of course the real problem is the time before people are treated, not how long a list is. In fact, due to the political environment in which health care operates, length of waiting lists is often quoted by the media and pressure groups trying to score points off each other, and consequently takes on an entirely artificial importance. Instead of being a means to an end, it can become an objective in its own right.

Are people complaining strongly about waiting time? If so it may be desirable to set up an enquiry which will at least give the impression that we care and are trying to improve matters. Whether we do or don't care, impressions are very important, and particularly so in a high profile political environment. Setting up an enquiry is also a traditional and effective way of delaying action while a political storm dies down following a disaster or policy decision. In the long-term, however, positive action will be required.

Is it desirable to make people wait? Some treatments are risky, and it may be important to ensure people have time to think about the possible outcomes, decide whether to have the treatment, and plan for the future. Some illnesses or complaints are best left for a while, often because they could cure themselves, so that they can ripen, or so that their severity can be determined and the extent of treatment determined. Situations like this should be taken out of our definition of waiting time.

Is the waiting time effectively a form of rationing? Politicians like to pretend that health care is not constrained by money, when in reality it is. Budgets are allocated for various types of treatment, and making people wait delays spending the money. Some people die while waiting, so this becomes a permanent saving!

Approaches that challenge assumptions include:
- Restricting the use of trained staff and other assets to those tasks that require them. Changing beds etc. carried out by general assistants, and teams of paramedics attending accidents in private cars or on motorbikes instead of ambulances. Using motorbikes might also result in their earlier arrival, resulting in faster commencement of treatment. The ambulance would still be sent, and have arrived by the time it was needed to transport the patient.

- DIY. Encourage patients to keep fit, take self-administered health checks and medicines at home, and only use the health services when they are genuinely ill. Better health education. Prevention is better than cure. Possibly give people a tax rebate if they have not been to the doctor in the previous year - could that be monitored?

- Not treating certain ailments / classes of people. At present, people are often given operations that have little chance of success, or drugs that will only keep them alive for a short time and in pain. While it would probably be political suicide to refuse treatment in given circumstances, allowing people to choose not to be treated may be acceptable. Euthanasia, under controlled conditions, is accepted practice in Holland.

- Encourage people to obtain treatment elsewhere e.g. private medicine, alternative approaches such as acupuncture and homeopathy, other EU countries. An extreme version of this is where some GPs are rumoured to be refusing to have sick or elderly people on their lists because they cost too much to treat!
- Resource allocation drag is a term I have already used to refer to the fact that budgets tend to be based on the previous year's spending, so new approaches have to be justified to a far greater extent than existing ones.

Zero based budgeting is a technique wherein budgets are started from scratch, attempts being made to allocate resources in the most effective way, not necessarily on those areas where the money was spent last year. A modern development on this line is Business Process Re-engineering, BPRE, which sets out to challenge existing methods.

BPRE can be encouraged, by preparing budgets on objective, rather than subjective, lines. Thus a budget would be set for 'treatment of stomach ulcers' rather than 'stomach operations'. This would mean, provided their assessment was performance based, budget holders would be encouraged to find new, efficient methods, as that would increase the number of patients treated.

Finally, to consider ways in which the length of the waiting list can be reduced for its own sake:

- Change the criteria for being placed on the list. Possibilities include not placing people on the list until they have been sick for six weeks; exclude those receiving any form of treatment, not in the country, who have moved recently etc., and stop keeping lists for certain treatments.

- Change the weighting given to particular types of treatment, so that those with short waiting lists (or even better, with currently long lists that can easily be reduced) have higher weightings. Weight the wait!

- Concentrate resources on those people on the lists that can be quickly treated, even though their needs, importance and urgency may be low.

- Be very careful to remove people from the list immediately they fail to qualify, conversely taking as long as possible to include people newly qualifying.

- Divide lists into two or more stages, treating each as a separate wait, thereby reducing average list time. Thus, someone could be placed on an assessment waiting list, once assessed they would go onto the treatment waiting list.
- Discourage patients from going on the list. Don't tell them the lists exist, discourage health checks so they remain unaware of their condition, make registration awkward by having complicated application forms asking for incredible details of personal and embarrassing information. If comparison is made between health organisations, and you are trying to make your organisation look good, encourage patients to register on a rival list instead of yours, improving your position and worsening your rival's!

While drawing up that list, I tried to be as cynical as possible: surely nobody would dream of doing such things? On re-reading it, however, I seem to recall several of the points made appearing in media stories. I know they tend to exaggerate to sell copy, but...

Logical

Appreciation / Specification

One way to cut waiting time would be to throw money at it i.e. spend more on health care. Another is to try to use the money more effectively. These two approaches are so different that it may be best to only consider one of them at a time. Should the problem be redefined as "How to cut waiting time for treatment within existing finance levels"?

Is there a need to act? How long are waiting lists, how accurate are they? We probably need to split the list geographically and for various treatments. Do they exist in all parts of the country, and for all problems? How long do people have to wait, and is this period growing? What would be an acceptable waiting time? Is the list kept and used in strict chronological order? If not, what selection criteria are used and how long is the maximum that patients wait?

To obtain this information, it will be necessary to measure the length of waiting lists and time people wait for various treatments, attempting to establish the accuracy of the information used. Are there people who need treatment but are not on waiting lists because they are not aware of their condition, have not registered, or due to administrative error or deliberate manipulation to artificially keep the list length down? On the other hand, some people may still be on the list who should not be e.g. they have been treated, the problem has cured itself, the person has moved or died. Individuals could be on two or more lists for the same treatment, either in error or in an attempt to ensure they are seen as soon as possible.

Why does it matter if people have to wait? Establish the effects waiting has, possibly using Cost Benefit Analysis: quantify the effects on all parties: pain, fear, loss of activity, loss of earnings, frustration, effect on relatives, employers and the economy, cost of coping pending final treatment e.g. drugs, dressings, consultations, monitoring. Deterioration could mean the eventual treatment costs far more than immediate action would have - possibly a literal illustration of the proverb a stitch in time saves nine!

Should we look at waiting time for various treatments? Accidents and emergencies should presumably take precedence over cosmetic surgery, but relative ranking would not be so clear in all cases.

Causes
- Too few resources (excluded from our investigation)

- Poor value for money (VFM)
    - ⇨ Uneconomic: paying too much for things
      * If we could obtain them cheaper, then we could have more for the same total cost

    - ⇨ Inefficient: not doing things right
      * Failure to obtain maximum use of our resources
      * Measures such as bed occupancy ratios can be calculated to reveal under-utilisation, but probably an even greater problem is ensuring that the most efficient form of treatment is used

- ⇨ Ineffective: not doing the right things
  * Do we carry out the right treatments, successfully?
  * Does the Health Service practice Right First Time philosophy?
  * It is often claimed that GPs are too busy to give proper consultations, and tend to prescribe drugs too readily. This fails to treat the cause and can result in long-term dependency, at great expense and no lasting benefit. The patient has to keep returning for further treatment and / or checks, thereby reducing resources available for others
  * Infection is often spread in hospitals, particularly mrsa (methicillin resistant staphylococcus aurius) following operations. Around 1 in 10 patients pick this up, treatment costs £1 billion a year, and about 5000 patients die from resultant fever and pneumonia

- Excessive, and unrealistic demand. The NHS was set up with the dream that once we treated people's ailments; they (the ailments and the people) would go away. This has proved to be wrong for several reasons
  - ⇨ Many ailments are not curable with existing knowledge, skill and treatments. They can, however, be kept in check using expensive resources
  - ⇨ Even if one ailment is cured, sooner or later people come back with another one
  - ⇨ Expectations keep growing. People expect free, fast, efficient treatment of all their health concerns; medical advances mean more ailments can be treated

- Treatments are becoming increasingly hi-tech, which often means high cost

- Waiting time may be accepted by some people as necessary and unavoidable for reasons covered above. This is more likely to be true of doctors than of patients, unless it is explained to them, which comes under Solutions / Implementation

Solutions
- Initially a brainstorm to generate a wide range of ideas.
  - Make doctors responsible for the resources they use, forcing them to become far more cost conscious. For example, when prescribing drugs they would be more inclined to use the cheapest effective version rather than a particular brand

  - Separate the provision of the service from the purchasing side, with hospitals free from close control by the Health Authority

  - Hospitals to compete in the provision of services, with GPs able to decide which hospital to send their patients to

  - Greater patient choice over what treatment they receive and where they obtain it, putting pressure on both GPs and hospitals to perform

  - Target maximum waiting times for various ailments / treatments

  - Ensure accurate performance measurement systems exist

  - Devise ways of comparing effectiveness of various treatments. This requires measuring the benefit received by the individual receiving the treatment, so is a form of Cost-Benefit Analysis

The concept of QALYs (Quality Adjusted Life Years) is of interest here. The quality and duration of the patient's life is judged, with and without the treatment. Results are compared to give the number of QALYs gained by the treatment, and relating this to cost can give a figure for cost per QALY, which can then be used to allocate resources. An example follows.

A person requiring a hip replacement may be judged to have a quality of life of 0.6 on a scale of 0.0 to 1.0. As the condition deteriorates, the quality of life would fall, say to 0.3 by the time the person died in, say 30 years time. Thus the person would have an expected 30 years at, say an average 0.45 i.e. 13.5 QALYs without the replacement.

If given the new hip, quality of life might improve to 0.9 and be expected to only fall to 0.7 over the 30 years. 30 years at 0.8 average gives 24 QALYs.

Increased QALYs if the hip is replaced are 24 - 13.5 = 10.5. If cost of treatment is £10,500 (net of any additional costs that would be necessary to care for the person if the operation did not take place) cost per QALY would be £1000

Costs per QALY of other activities could be calculated and relative rankings produced

Clearly, there are many problems with the above process. Is it possible to objectively assess people's quality of life? To what extent will it depend on the transplant? Who decides, the doctor or individual? Would you like to tell someone they couldn't have an operation because the cost per QALY is too high? Can the costs of treatment (and non-treatment) be accurately determined? Can spin off benefits (e.g. increased knowledge and experience gained by doctors) be assessed and allowed for? When heart transplants were first performed, they were extremely expensive and produced relatively few QALYs, now costs are falling and QALYs rising.

Despite these problems, the concept of QALYs is interesting and valuable. If demand for health care exceeds supply, as many people believe it invariably does, priority decisions have to be taken. Without a logical approach such as QALYs, such decisions will be taken in secret and on an arbitrary basis.

Two particular approaches to solving the problem are now considered in more detail:
> Improve utilisation of assets
> Use the most efficient form of treatment

Improve Utilisation of Assets
Benchmarking is a technique in which the performances achieved by various organisations are compared with each other, then attempts are made to establish the reasons why the top performing ones are better than the others. The poor performers can then try to copy their methods, thereby improving their own performance. Calculation and comparison of bed occupancy ratios, for example, would be followed by comparison of methods and a search for ways in which the ratios could be improved. Possibilities include careful scheduling of operations so that those requiring four day's recovery are done on Mondays, two day's on Wednesday, and day cases on Fridays, thereby enabling the ward to be closed for the weekend, and saving running costs.

Time spent in hospital after the event is another potential area for improvement, it being realised that in addition to the cost savings, many patients in fact recover faster in their own homes, and stand less risk of catching mrsa. The Government's move towards Community Care is an example of this, with patients being moved from hospitals and long-stay accommodation back into the community, either in residential accommodation or in their own or relatives' homes.

Use the Most Efficient Form of Treatment
Many new forms of treatment exist which are extremely efficient and effective, including those known collectively as minimal invasion surgery such as ultrasound and lasers.
Minor operations can be done under local anaesthetic, enabling a day patient approach. An extreme variation which uses the Mind Games concept of challenging assumptions, and was mentioned in chapter 5, is the conveyor belt adopted in Russia for eye cataract operations: instead of the medical team moving to the patient, patients sit on chairs which pass the medical team.

Prevention is better, and often far cheaper, than cure, so the possibility of encouraging people to look after themselves, by e.g. subsidising their gym membership fee, should be considered.

Having generated a number of possible solutions, it is necessary to select those for implementation. In the case under consideration, most are compatible with each other, the main exception being that measures aimed purely at reducing the length of the list do tend to conflict with those aimed at genuinely tackling waiting time / value for money.

Selection depends on available resources, time and ease of implementation, and assessment of the likely costs and benefits from each suggestion. Involvement of others in the selection process helps ensure their commitment.

Groups
Who shall we involve in the decision? Doctors, nurses, academics, politicians (local and national), representatives from user groups? Setting up a committee would give all these people a chance to contribute, but would also greatly lengthen the process. It would also mean that the decision would be made by a majority of the members, which might not be desirable.

Given the scale of the Health Service, it is possible to test ideas in particular locations before full adoption, using champions and particularly suitable facilities, including highly skilled staff.
It is particularly important to gain acceptance of doctors, nurses and the patients of any changes, since without their agreement any proposals are likely to fail.

Political implications of solutions require consideration, as do hidden agendas such as doctors protecting their self-employed status and freedom to work outside the NHS. The opposition is always on the look-out for signs of failure to achieve immediate improvements, which reduces the possibility of adopting a long-term view . Doom mongers abound, as do rumours of poor treatment.

Unfortunately, several very bad episodes have come to light. The mass murderer Doctor Shipman is the most notorious, but misinterpretation of scan results and a few fatal errors in administering drugs are other examples. The media and opposition latch onto these, exaggerate their scale and effects, and public image and faith are badly damaged. Staff morale is claimed to be falling, but it is difficult to accurately judge the validity of such claims due to the previously mentioned factors.

Partly in an attempt to counteract such hostile publicity, a great deal of attention is given to "selling" changes in the NHS, highlighting the benefits to the various parties, including more interesting jobs and healthier lives.

Proper training and financing of solutions is required, and frequent checking of progress, ensuring forces in favour of change always prevail.

Implementation
- The government has prepared several White Papers on the subject of health. A tremendous amount of consultation has taken place, and comments invited.

- Targets have been established for waiting list levels, and detailed guidance provided on how they can be reduced. A Committee for Health Improvement has been established with the remit of identifying and encouraging use of the most efficient forms of treatment.

- Plans and programmes have been developed, discussed and put in motion. Conferences have been held to discuss implementation.

- Implementation is still taking place, the nature of the problem being that continuous effort is required. Specific actions include most of the methods suggested above:

- Doctors are being made more directly responsible for the resources they use, through the introduction of GP budgets and Primary Care Groups (PCGs)

- Provision of the service has been largely separated from the purchasing side, with hospitals becoming Trusts, and free of direct control by the Health Authority

- Hospitals are being required to compete with each other in the provision of services, with GPs and PCGs able to decide which hospital to send their patients to

- Greater patient's choice is being encouraged as to what treatment they receive and where they obtain it

- Performance measurement systems and ways of comparing effectiveness of various treatments are being introduced and constantly refined

- Utilisation of assets is constantly monitored and ways to improve efficiency tested, including reduction in recovery times and optimum use of the day patient approach
- General assistants are being used to change beds and do other low skill tasks

- Emphasis is being placed on health education, the importance of people keeping fit and having regular health checks. A national help line has been set up to help people diagnose themselves and to only use the health services when they are genuinely ill

- Private health care is being encouraged, as are alternative approaches such as homeopathy, although doctors vary in their attitude towards treatments like acupuncture

- Business process re-engineering has taken place to a surprisingly high extent, with new forms of treatment being given strong support

Review
This requires comparison of waiting lists before and after implementation, and with target lengths.

Difficulties include increasing demand levels, effects of epidemics and seasonal factors, allowing for time lags between implementation of new ideas and their taking effect, and the complexities caused by scale. Definition of waiting lists, their importance and validity as a performance measure, and geographical variations, are each important.

Publication of national results have shown that despite all efforts and increased spending (outside our scope, but clearly a major influence) overall length of waiting lists has not changed much during the last decade. Speed of treatment and chance of success depends very much on one's postcode! Even so, given the vastly increased level of demand, maintaining lists at their earlier levels could be viewed as a worthwhile achievement.

Learn
The final stage in the problem solving process is attempting to learn from the experience.

An immediate conclusion would be that reducing waiting lists is a poor objective. You may recall my use of the mnemonic SMART in the answer to one of the exercises at the end of chapter 2: objectives should be Specific, Measurable, Achievable, Relevant and Time-related. Reducing waiting lists fails on several counts. It is difficult to define or measure, can be manipulated, and can lead to focusing on the wrong activities, ailments and patients. The length of the lists becomes an end, rather than a means to an end. We should be attempting to optimise health levels, and length of waiting lists is only one element of the problem / solution.

It is probably true to say that there has been a dramatic increase in activity levels, but expectations keep growing, and are already unrealistic, given the palliative nature of many treatments, and increasing longevity and quality of life. Increasingly open debate is taking place of policies such as euthanasia due to the amount of money spent on people who are in pain and cannot be cured.

Due to its political nature, the truth is hard to ascertain. All parties tend to cloud the issues, focusing on aspects that suit them, and dodging others. Labour, for example, having been in power for four years, still claimed that to be too short a period to expect them to have turned round the situation left them by the previous administration.

Value for money is hard to assess. Great attention has been given to the efficiency aspect, ensuring high levels of asset utilisation, but an area in which I feel the Health Service, and public sector in general, could make great improvements is that of effectiveness. Too many mistakes are made, drugs still prescribed too easily, and the situation regarding MRSA, previously outlined, is extremely worrying.

This is the end of the book, but hopefully only the beginning of your improved decision making! Please apply it to the final question!

In chapter 1, I expressed the hope that you would enjoy the book and find it useful and thought-provoking. If you did, tell your friends; if not, congratulations on your staying power!

Self Test Questions

7.1 For the last time, what are the seven stages in logical decision making?

7.2 How do magical and group aspects fit in?

7.3 What are the three elements of VFM?

7.4 Give four reasons why demand for health care is effectively limitless

7.5 What are QALYs? Give 6 problems with their use

7.6 Is the real problem length of waiting lists, or waiting time?

7.7 What parties should be involved in decisions about reducing hospital waiting lists?

7.8 How can the Resource Allocation Drag problem be tackled?

7.9 Can you suggest four additional solutions to the waiting time problem?

Exercises

7.1 Under what circumstances would you decide not to involve other people in your decision making?

7.2 Carry out an in-depth analysis of the problem 'Getting to Fires / Accidents'.

If possible, involve other people at various stages, e.g. carrying out a brainstorming exercise to generate solutions.

7.3 Consider some of the major changes in your life / work:
- Which were "your" changes, which were "other people's"?
- How did you feel about them at the time (e.g. worried, out of control, pleased, sure of results)?
- What was it about each change that made you feel that way?
- Did your feelings prove justified?
- Would you welcome further similar changes?

(No answer is provided for this exercise)

7.4 The Final Problem!
It has just been realised that the earth will be hit by a major catastrophe in the near future, and has been many times in the past. Once every 15,000 years or so, a super-volcano explodes, virtually wiping out civilisation.

Scientists have discovered a major build-up beneath much of North America, covering the whole of the Yellowstone National Park and surrounding regions. The build-up consists of a vast cavern of molten rock, topped by billions of cubic metres of super-heated water, and capped by a relatively thin crust of solid rock, to complete a giant pressure cooker. As the molten rock continues to rise from within the earth's core, it will eventually force the solid rock cap up. Once the cap lifts sufficiently to allow contact with the atmosphere, the water will start to vaporise, causing the cap to explode. This will trigger an immense explosion as the remaining water and much of the molten rock vaporises. Global devastation will follow.

Measurements have discovered that the cap is rising, and estimates vary from 10 to 150 years before it explodes. Evidence has been found of similar events stretching back through geological history, coinciding with recognised periods of mass destruction of animal species.

What should we do?

Governments are already planning to send some people into space, possibly to live on the moon or in an orbiting space station. Additionally, nuclear bunker-type dwellings are being built.

In addition to searching for ways to ensure we survive, means are being sought whereby we can leave a warning to the descendants of any survivors, who may well go through a complete disintegration of civilisation. If there were no survivors, we would still want to warn any intelligent life forms which either visit from other worlds, or ultimately evolve to create a new civilisation, so that they can take evasive action at an earlier stage. It is hoped to include detailed information about us, and a full set of our knowledge.

Some initial thoughts are that we should try to build structures that will survive both the coming disaster, and for many thousands of years into the future. We could either place the information in them, or use them as pointers to where it can be found (e.g. points of a cross) although this latter idea has the obvious weakness that if one structure is destroyed, the plan fails.

We could try an 'obvious' location, say on top of the highest mountain, or middle of the largest ocean, or a unique geographical feature (Ayres Rock in the centre of Australia?), or use such features as pointers. At the same time, however, the information must be somewhere / something difficult to find so that it is not destroyed or accidentally ruined by descendants insufficiently developed to understand or use it. Ways must be found to protect it from such users, while still enabling the sophisticated ultimate target users to recognise and access it.

Thinking about the situation facing us has encouraged people to consider whether this problem has been faced by earlier civilisations, and whether their attempts at passing down their warnings and knowledge to us are still awaiting our discovery and / or recognition. Is this the true secret of the Sphinx, Pyramids (Egyptian and Mayan), Easter Island statues, and Stonehenge? Are there secrets within or beneath such structures that we should be seeking out? Was Ayres Rock deliberately placed in the centre of Australia as an obvious signpost?

Were some of their structures or pointers either destroyed or very badly damaged? By luck or judgement, are pyramids the ideal shape for withstanding major catastrophes and the ravages of time? Did our ancestors deliberately choose natural materials to lessen the chance of deliberate destruction by a developing civilisation? Did they use building scales and techniques that would be recognised as obviously highly advanced to an advanced civilisation? Did they leave certain artefacts and information to encourage the development of religions whose real purpose (hidden even from their leaders) was to protect the chosen sites? Are the religions more powerful than our ancestors predicted, causing us to continue to treat the sites as sacred even now are?

Have some of the items left been found and not recognised for what they truly are? In 1900, fragments of an encrusted bronze 'machine', including more than twenty gearwheels and engraved scales, were found, and later dated to the first century BC. The assumption has been made that they belonged to an ancient 'computer' used to determine the motions of celestial bodies. A tribe in Mali had a mythology that the star Sirius actually consisted of two stars, one orbiting the other: this has now been proved to be correct. Ancient maps have been found showing feature which cannot have been known to the cartographers e.g. the shape of the coastline underneath thousands of feet of ice in Antarctica.

This then, is the final problem: How can we ensure our information survives even if we don't, and is received by our descendants, in whatever form they take? How can we find the information left by earlier civilisations, if such exists?

Solution will take logic, magic, group work, and a factor not mentioned in the book: luck!

I have deliberately left the problem and my initial thoughts vague, as I do not want to restrict the thought processes of those attempting to find solutions.

I view this as the most important question facing humanity, and a fitting test of your ability to apply the ideas contained within the book. Go for it!

Needless to say, I do not provide an answer to this final problem.

Answers to Exercises

7.1 Other people should not be involved in decision making if:

Advantages of involvement low
Little need for specialist knowledge; no need to generate solutions or debate viability; no concern over adverse behavioural aspects; others will not be involved in nor affected by implementation; importance of decision low; consequences of error low; scope limited.

Decision known
No real decision; only requires calculation or solving of mathematical formulae, and you have the required skill.

Costs of involvement excessive or not available
Time, money, effort.

Deliberate exclusion
Avoid ideas you do not want considered; concern over their hidden agendas; decision too contentious; fear of leaks or friction; avoid others thinking you are unable to make decisions alone; influence of powerful individuals; desire for personal glory; avoid frustration of individuals whose ideas are rejected.

Lack of suitable people:
Unbalanced group e.g. regarding level of experience and negotiation skills, hence fear of bias or domination by individuals.

Communication problems:
Geographical separation; different backgrounds, experiences, knowledge or beliefs; parlo solo Italiano.

7.2 Getting to Fires / Accidents

Mind Games

Why go?
Get someone else to go! Transfer risk - privatise

Who are we? What is our role?
Fire brigade / police / ambulance?
Media, on-lookers, lawyers, break down firm?
Is our current role the right one? Could it be better done by another group?

Is 'getting there' the real problem?
Or is it receiving notification, or what we do once there?

Getting what to fires / accidents?
Water, first-aid, other equipment (ladders, pumps, hoses, RTA gear)?
An individual, a team, skill, knowledge?
Could some of these be achieved in new ways e.g. using mobiles?
Is it necessary to take water? To RTAs? Would another approach be more effective e.g. foam, sand, massive fire blankets to cover buildings?!

Do fires and accidents require entirely different approaches?
Different personnel, equipment, locations

'To' the fire?
Or to where it will be? (forest fires spread rapidly)
How close?

Should we concentrate on prevention?
Would it be better not to fight fires at all? No risk to fire fighters, does water cause more damage than the fires? concentrate on preventing spread (protect nearby buildings, remove flammable material).
Does an improvement to accident arrival / treatment speed lead to individuals being less careful?
There are relatively few fires, so concentrate on RTAs.

Business Process Re-engineering
Go for hi-tec solutions
Automatic alarms e.g. could mobile phones, cameras or sensors detect and report accidents?
Is water still the best approach?
Why do fire engines always seem to come from behind the incident, fighting their way through the jammed traffic? There is no traffic in front of the incident! This approach would seem particularly relevant on dual carriageways and motorways
More variety of approaches e.g. use of individuals on motorbikes to achieve fast arrival and start assessing situation

Logical

Appreciation / Specification

What stages in the process are we interested in?
Incident starts - alarm - communication - set out - journey - arrival - act - effective - return

What types of fire / accident are we interested in?
Only 'out of control', significant danger to life or property, in certain geographical area?
How often do they occur, when and where?
What effects do they have e.g. loss of life / property?

How long does it take to get to them now?
What would constitute success?
Fewer fires / accidents, faster arrival? I will assume concern is about speed of reaction / arrival, but that takes out all aspects such as prevention.
How quickly is a solution needed e.g. are we reacting to a spate of fires, one major disaster, or a general concern about effectiveness?

Do any models / numerical approaches exist
To analyse e.g. traffic flows, effect of various sirens?
Should we involve experts e.g. Fire Brigade / Ambulance Service?
Has research already been carried out?

When and where are the delays?
How and why do they occur?
How soon do we know once an incident occurs?
Are messages clear and precise?
Do we interpret them correctly?
Why do we take so long to react now?
Is there considerable delay en route?

Causes
Few alarms
Lack of telephones / other communication methods
Lack of concern / awareness / reaction: assume 'someone else will ring'
Location of emergency equipment / personnel
Speed of reaction by us - asleep, getting going
Machine breakdown / crashes
Speed / flexibility of machines
Traffic hold-ups - volume, stupid actions by drivers trying to get out of the way, lights and other road crossing hazards
No access route - not near a road

Solutions
Educate the general public to fight their own fires, treat accident victims, and notify us of incidents;
Legal requirement to carry first aid equipment and fire extinguishers on all vehicles
Sprinkler systems / fire doors etc. so that role of emergency services is carried out automatically i.e. no need to arrive!
More alarms / telephones (mobiles are having a great effect on speed of notification) / CCTV cameras;
Reward those first to scene (too much competition could cause various units to sabotage each other, or more crashes en route)
More equipment, located closer to known trouble spots
Locate machines on fast routes
Prioritise e.g. traffic light override controls
Variety of machines / equipment: some small, highly mobile to achieve fast arrival and initiate action (e.g. motorcycle medics), others larger and more fully equipped, but likely to take longer to arrive

Groups
Look out for:
Attempts at blame shifting / avoidance
Manipulation of figures to disguise true performance
Hostility to solutions, and attempts to undermine implementation
Media hype? Over-reaction to a few high profile late arrivals
Hidden agendas - loss of status or team spirit

Force Field Analysis
Develop forces for change
Analyse existing forces
Generate concern, enthusiasm and commitment
Look for some high ranking champions
Keep pushing

'Sell' Solutions
Genuine problem, which can be successfully tackled
Involve other emergency services and pressure groups:
Insurance / breakdown assistance companies, victim support

Easy result areas first
Any known weak areas where change will be welcomed by all
Trials with keen groups

Implementation
To implement those ideas decided upon would require full backing and agreement of senior management. An individual should be placed in overall charge and held responsible for achieving implementation.

Plans and programmes would have to be produced, stating responsibilities, prioritising developments, setting targets and key results.

Any required changes in structure, activities, processes, rules and contracts would have to be introduced.

Careful communication of the changes taking place, their justification, and requirements on individuals would be necessary. Training, both courses and 'on the job' would be required to reinforce the change, ensure thorough understanding, and deal with any practical issues.

Review / Learn
These two stages cannot really be done in a hypothetical scenario analysis since no implementation has taken place and any relevant points would have been included in earlier sections.

As discussed above, there probably are opportunities for improvement in areas such as communication and transportation. A particular concern would be whether the thinking is flexible, fundamentally challenging, and sufficiently aware of modern developments. These are all areas shown throughout the book to be extremely important in modern business decision making.

Such thoughts would lead us back into the appreciation and specification stages, which is where we came in! Feel free to start again at page 1.